1968

1968

THOSE WERE THE DAYS
BRIAN WILLIAMS

The
History
Press

Remembering my father, whose heart
sank that year most Saturdays, but whose
optimism never wavered.

First published 2017

The History Press
The Mill, Brimscombe Port
Stroud, Gloucestershire, GL5 2QG
www.thehistorypress.co.uk

British Library Cataloguing in Publication Data.
A catalogue record for this book is available from the British Library.

ISBN 978 0 7509 8430 0

Typesetting and origination by The History Press
Printed and bound in Great Britain by TJ International Ltd

Contents

Introduction

'DON'T MAKE IT BAD ...'

'Hey Jude', sang the Beatles, whose Apple Corps launched a boutique shop offering psychedelic fashion at psychedelic prices. 'The Fab Four', still together, topped the charts yet again with the refrain that lingered long into the summer night, 'Don't make it bad, take a sad song and make it better'.

There were sad songs aplenty in 1968, but some cheer as well, and many people trying to make the situation better. It was the year when humans first glimpsed the far side of the Moon, but also the year the world was shocked by assassination, by the crushing of hope for reform and by wars that showed no sign of ever ending. To the old there seemed too much change, too quickly, with 'youth' in revolt, though against what no one was entirely sure, except that the word 'freedom' was repeatedly used.

Britain was surprisingly different in 1968, although some things never change: a government battling with the economy; austerity; self-questioning about Britain's role in the world, in or out of Europe. How to get on with the Americans? And the Russians? And, of course, the French? Issues in the media were depressingly familiar: immigration, censorship, crime ('watch out, there's a thief about'). Northern Ireland's Troubles were brewing. Foreigners were buying up London real estate, in this case a symbolic piece – London Bridge – sold to an American businessman, to be dismantled stone by stone and re-erected in Arizona. The *Queen Elizabeth*, Cunard's pride, was also sold, and faced an uncertain future. People lost their money – the old sort – and gained some shiny new coins – the 5p and 10p pieces; there was news that the 'ten-bob note' (10 shillings) would also soon be gone, replaced by a seven-sided coin (50p). Yet, even after the 1967 devaluation crisis, people were, on the whole, feeling better off – this was, after all, the 'Swinging Sixties'. And they were being urged to 'back Britain', eagerly promoting itself as the land of Carnaby Street, miniskirts and 'with-it' cool.

In 1968, the UK population was just over 55 million. There were more than 12 million motor vehicles and about the same number of telephones, all connected to land lines, though many people needing to make a call still faced a walk to the nearest public telephone box. There were no mobiles, no smartphones, no Facebook, Google or Twitter. The term 'social media' would have meant little and 'Amazon' was a very big river. Barbecues were what Americans and Australians had, and a takeaway almost always meant fish and chips, though the more daring could get an Indian or Chinese meal, or even a pizza, though this was probably only in London, where a Pizza Express had been open for just three years. Radio licences (still required) were held for 18 million households; slightly fewer homes (15 million) had television licences. In winter, most families sat around an open coal fire burning British fuel. Britain's mines produced more than 160 million tons of coal a year. People took a bath, not a shower. Recent changes in building regulations had suggested the urgency of reducing heat loss, but in the late 1960s hardly any houses had double glazing.

So what was new? Concorde was new, and America's jumbo jet, the Boeing 747. The Ford Escort was new, as was crossing the Channel by hovercraft. Tower blocks were newish, never really popular and even less so after a block of flats in London collapsed following a gas explosion. The Beatles flew off to India to meditate on peace and love; other bands and fans headed for Hyde Park or the Isle of Wight for a taste of a new experience – an outdoor pop concert/festival. Louis Armstrong sang of a 'wonderful world'; it was certainly one in transition.

The Swinging Sixties were reshaping society, in sexual politics and marriage, as well as in fashion, but with change came unrest – industrial, economic, sectarian, racial and generational. Riots and protest made the news. Full of ideas, fervour and angry words, students marched, sat down and sat in, from the Sorbonne to Prague, in London's Grosvenor Square and across America. The world's superpower, already experiencing inner turmoil over civil rights and the Vietnam War, was in 1968 shaken by the murders of Martin Luther King Jr and Robert F. Kennedy.

But revolution? Maybe next year, though it had already happened on stage. No more censorship, let it all hang out. And it did in *Hair*, the hippie musical with lights, music, naked action, four-letter words and audience participation. Meanwhile, a right-on commuter could show right-on radical leanings by carrying, or reading, *Couples*, *Last Exit to Brooklyn*, *Sexual Politics*, or *No More Fun and Games: A Journal of Female Liberation*. For the family, there was a new programme on television, *Dad's Army*, and much more to amuse or ponder on. John Lennon and Yoko Ono sat in a white bag at the Royal Albert Hall for their 'Alchemical Wedding' event; Britain narrowly failed to win the Eurovision Song Contest with 'Congratulations'; NASA sent Apollo 8 around the Moon and Gary Sobers smashed 36 runs in an over by scoring six sixes. It was an Olympic year, too.

It was a good year for Matt Busby, knighted after Manchester United won the European Cup; for Alec Rose, also knighted following his round-the-world voyage; and for long jumper Bob Beamon, whose gold medal at the Mexico Olympics was secured with a record-shattering leap through thinning air. It was a good year, too, for Cecil Day-Lewis, who became Poet Laureate in succession to John Masefield; for Colin Davis (new director of the Royal Opera House); for Trevor Nunn (new head of the Royal Shakespeare Company); and for George Best, Europe's footballer of the year. A year to remember also for Virginia Wade, winner of the US Open tennis title, as the distinction between amateur and professional tennis was abolished. And when the twelve months were almost over, Leonid Brezhnev could pat himself on the back for clawing back the Czechs with the iron grasp of Soviet power. Richard Nixon could look at the mirror and smile, in the knowledge that he had finally made it to the White House. Harold Wilson could congratulate himself on still being in Number 10; George Brown could only wonder where it had all gone wrong. The weather was typically mixed: some unusually severe thunderstorms, floods, and parts of the country turned reddish-brown by sand blown in from the Sahara (the experts said); the summer was on the whole disappointingly dull, cool and damp for those seeking a healthy (it was still thought) suntan. An end-of-year bonus came for parts of the country: a white Christmas. And next year, the Americans promised, man would walk on the Moon ...

Timeline

JANUARY

5   Alexander Dubček becomes new Communist Party leader in Czechoslovakia

8   Prime Minister Harold Wilson announces support for the 'I'm Backing Britain' campaign to boost the economy (suggestions include buying British and working half an hour a day without pay)

21   A US B-52 bomber crashes in Greenland, with nuclear weapons on board

23   USS *Pueblo* and eighty-three crew seized by North Korea

30   In the Vietnam War, the Vietcong launch their 'Tet Offensive' in South Vietnam

FEBRUARY

10   10th Winter Olympic Games begin at Grenoble in France

16   The Beatles and others – including Mia Farrow and Donovan – visit India to see Maharishi Mahesh Yogi

MARCH

1   *Joseph and the Amazing Technicolor Dreamcoat*, by Andrew Lloyd Webber and Tim Rice, gets a first sung hearing at a London school

15 Foreign Secretary George Brown resigns, ending his career at the top of British Labour Party politics

12 Mauritius gains independence after 158 years of British rule

17 Anti-Vietnam War protesters pack London's Grosvenor Square to mob the US Embassy; injuries and arrests result as violence breaks out

27 Russian cosmonaut Yuri Gagarin is killed when his plane crashes

APRIL

4   Civil rights leader Martin Luther King Jr is shot dead in Memphis, USA

7   Scottish racing driver Jim Clark is killed at Hockenheim, in Germany, when his Lotus leaves the track and hits a tree

18 London Bridge, dating from 1831, is sold to an American businessman, who wants to rebuild it stone by stone in Arizona. It 'reopens' at Lake Havasu City in 1971

22 Britain's first 'Open' tennis event, the Hard Courts Championship at Bournemouth

23 New 5p and 10p decimal coins make their debuts

29 Broadway's new musical *Hair* shocks audiences when cast members strip naked on stage

MAY

4   Mary Hopkin sings on TV's *Opportunity Knocks*, and is recommended to Paul McCartney

16 Ronan Point, a London tower block, partially collapses following a gas explosion in a resident's kitchen

18 In the FA Cup Final, West Bromwich Albion's Dennis Clark is the first substitute ever to get on the pitch in a final

22 The US nuclear submarine *Scorpion* is lost in the Atlantic Ocean, with a crew of ninety-nine. It is one of four submarines (the others are Israeli, Russian and French) lost during the year

29 Manchester United are the first English soccer club to win the European Cup, beating Benfica of Portugal at Wembley

JUNE

1 Helen Keller, blind and deaf from the age of 18 months, who became famous as author, lecturer and inspiration, dies at the age of 87

5 Bobby Kennedy is shot in a Los Angeles hotel while campaigning for the US presidency, and dies next day

10 NHS prescription charges are reintroduced, having been abolished in Britain in 1965

25 Comedian Tony Hancock commits suicide in Australia

JULY

4 Lone yachtsman Alec Rose sails home to Portsmouth after a solo circumnavigation lasting 354 days

6 Billie Jean King (USA) wins the women's singles title at the first 'Open' Wimbledon tennis tournament

25 In his encyclical *Humanae Vitae*, Pope Paul VI tells Roman Catholics they must not practise birth control

AUGUST

1 New hovercraft passenger service begins between Dover and Boulogne

11 British Rail runs its last steam-hauled passenger trains, charging enthusiasts more than £15 for the privilege

20 Warsaw Pact troops and tanks invade Czechoslovakia to crush the reform movement begun under the leadership of Alexander Dubček

22 In Chicago, USA, police clash with anti-war protesters at the Democratic Party Convention
24 France tests its first hydrogen bomb
31 West Indies cricketer Gary Sobers hits six sixes in one over for Nottinghamshire against Glamorgan at Swansea, the unlucky bowler being Malcolm Nash

SEPTEMBER

6 Swaziland in Africa becomes an independent kingdom within the Commonwealth
16 The Post Office's new two-tier system introduces first- and second-class stamps
17 The MCC cricket tour of South Africa is cancelled after the South African apartheid regime refuses to accept Basil D'Oliveira as a member of the England party
27 Portugal's dictator António Salazar steps down after thirty-six years as prime minister

OCTOBER

9 Harold Wilson holds talks with Rhodesia's Ian Smith aboard HMS *Fearless*, but fails to find a resolution of the crisis caused by the colony's white minority government's unilateral declaration of independence
11 US spacecraft Apollo 7 is launched with three astronauts – the first manned test flight of the Apollo Moon craft
12 The Olympic Games begin in Mexico City; the Games are marked by a spate of world records and 'Black Power' demonstrations by US athletes
23 The Cunard liner *Queen Elizabeth* sails from Southampton on her final passenger-carrying crossing to New York, before being retired to Florida as a hotel
20 British Crazy Gang comedian Bud Flanagan dies; his last recording is 'Who Do You Think You are Kidding, Mr Hitler?' for the BBC's *Dad's Army*

20 Jacqueline Kennedy, widow of the late President Kennedy, marries Greek shipping tycoon Aristotle Onassis
24 The US X-15 rocket plane retires after setting several flight records, including a 1967 speed record of Mach 6.72 (4,534mph/7,927km/h)
31 President Johnson announces that the United States will stop its air and other attacks on North Vietnam

NOVEMBER

5 Richard Nixon wins the US presidential election, beating his Democrat rival Hubert Humphrey
22 The Beatles' 'White Album' (officially *The Beatles*) is released
28 Children's writer Enid Blyton (*Noddy*, *Famous Five* …) dies

DECEMBER

17 Mary Bell (11) is sentenced to life imprisonment for killing two small boys in Newcastle upon Tyne
20 Nobel Laureate writer John Steinbeck dies in New York City
21 The Apollo 8 spacecraft is launched. With three astronauts aboard, it flies around the Moon and back, orbiting the Moon on Christmas Eve
30 Death of Trygve Lie, Norwegian diplomat and the UN's first secretary general (1946–52)
31 Russia announces the first flight of the Tu-144, the world's first supersonic airliner, which pips the Anglo-French Concorde as the first supersonic transport in the air

1

January

BACKING BRITAIN

The good times are blowing our way ...

A new year brings new resolutions. The start of 1968 marked the launch of the 'I'm Backing Britain' campaign, begun by five office workers in Surbiton who were willing, they said, to give up half an hour's pay a day to help the country out of its economic difficulties. Newspapers scented a five-minute wonder. Prime Minister Harold Wilson (never one knowingly to miss a media trick) declared his support for the flag-waving campaign: buy British and save the pound. So did millionaire publisher Robert Maxwell, but he wanted his own slogan. Up sprouted carrier bags emblazoned with Union flags; on went T-shirts claiming the wearer was 'Backing Britain' (some were made in Portugal, but then the Portuguese were our oldest allies). Bruce Forsyth did his bit for the movement by recording the eponymous song, written by Tony Hatch and Jackie Trent. Its lyrics included the optimistic line 'the good times are blowing our way'. Perhaps they were, but it took a little time.

While wandering up and down the high street (which most town centres retained in the mid-1960s), patriotic shoppers could take comfort from the thought that much being sold in the shops bore a 'Made in Britain' label. This was true especially of clothes. The latest rag trade fashions were British, even if outsourced for manufacture, and high-street icons such as Marks & Spencer could still claim that their clothing was made in Britain. In much of the fashion trade, traditional styles prevailed, though in more 'modern' materials, such as Terylene, while the shrinking length of women's skirts meant more minis per square yard of fabric. For those backing Britain whose dress was neither 'mod' nor 'hippie', a conventionally styled suit or tweed sports jacket could be theirs from a high-street tailors' store. A man's tweed jacket cost 7 guineas from Dunn & Co.; the guinea (21 shillings, equivalent to 105p today) remained the popular retail way to pricing items such as clothes and furniture.

Harold Wilson was not about to swap his Gannex raincoat for a psychedelic kaftan, but his government saw no reason why pop and patriotism should not unite to boost the economy. Amid the psychedelia in shop windows, on album covers and posters, an outbreak of Union flags and slogans urging people to 'Back Britain' might seem incongruous, but the message could be woven into most media, with a little imagination. The Union flag was cool enough to be applied anywhere, and 'backing Britain' became almost a dummy run for 'cool Britannia'.

'Backing Britain' at least sounded positive, at a time when Prime Minister Wilson was trying to restore his reputation for financial acumen following the 1967 decision to devalue the pound. Then, doing his best to sound like Stanley Baldwin, the prime minister had appeared before the British public puffing his pipe and earnestly assuring them that the 'pound in their pocket' was worth the same after devaluation. Few believed him.

Another cloud gathering on the monetary horizon was decimalisation. The devalued pound in purse (or pocket) was still a pound, a paper note rustling among an assortment of familiar jingling coins – shillings and pence. But change was coming. Politicians had decreed that the country would go decimal, a change three years away, but already evident. In the twilight of its long history, dating from the late 1400s, the shilling still reigned, but alongside an upstart twin – the new 5p coin that first appeared in 1968. As did a larger 10p piece, which people were told was the same as a 2-shilling piece (the florin). Since every child knew there were 12 pennies in a shilling (not 5), and 24 pennies in 2 shillings (not 10), many viewed the interlopers, and forthcoming decimalisation, with suspicion.

High-street banks were changing too. The local bank was a landmark of solidity in towns across the country. Most people with bank accounts called there at least once a week, if only to cash a cheque. There were no plastic cards, and Britain's first cash machine was just a year old. The bank was familiar and trusted, unaltered on the outside for decades and little changed inside. Typical high streets had four or five, as well as the larger building societies. Then in 1968 two of the old familiar names, National Provincial and Westminster, announced an amalgamation to create a bigger bank, NatWest. The famous grasshopper sign of another bank, Martins, was also shortly to disappear, gobbled up by Barclays in 1969.

To watch the news and see how the 'Backing Britain' campaign was doing, families could rent a colour television for 25s a week. Rental TV was a popular alternative to purchase, for television sets, still somewhat temperamental, were liable to go wrong and require the attention of a technician. Time in many households was spent twiddling knobs to adjust the picture. The advent of colour TV in 1967 had been a boon to manufacturers and advertisers alike, but in 1968 only one channel (BBC2) was transmitting programmes in colour. BBC1 and ITV followed in 1969.

'Backing Britain' by buying British was all very well, but the country still faced a major problem with its balance of trade, and trade figures were seldom out of the headlines. Today's financial barometers tend to focus on 'consumer confidence' (retail sales) and credit debt. In 1968 everyone worried about the trade gap, and with Britain's imports (£7.9 billion) exceeding exports (£6.4 billion), there was much political wrangling about trade and industrial performance. Labour's ambitious National Plan was now minus its leader, George Brown. Having departed Economic Affairs for the Foreign Office, Brown was in 1968 about to say goodbye to government for good. To kick-start economic growth, the government sponsored regional economic development councils, nicknamed 'Little Neddies', after the National Economic Development Council ('Big Neddy') which had been around since 1962, supposedly to plan industrial strategy. These hung on without much consequence until scrapped by the Major government in 1992.

Machinery, motor vehicles and chemicals were key foreign trade earners for Britain, followed by textiles. Financial services, today so crucial to national income and tax receipts, made few headlines, and 'banker-bashing' even fewer: finance in the public conception of how the economy worked mattered far less than manufacturing, shipbuilding, steel-making or coal mining. In the 1960s City traders were often old-school gents in suits, whose use of technology was restricted to tickertape machines and telephones. Financial transactions relied largely on mechanical equipment, though electronic tickers were being introduced. The first awkward steps towards computerised trading were being made, but the trading floor was still largely in the hands of humans, at least for another year or so; all this would begin to change in the 1970s.

Patterns of trade were shifting too. In the late 1960s, the UK's main trade destination for exports was the European Economic Community (EEC), or the Common Market as it was generally known. Euro-trade accounted for about 20 per cent of exports; yet Britain was not a member of the six-nation European club. Efforts to join the Common Market had begun under the Conservatives in 1961, but when the Macmillan government applied for membership, its overtures were rebuffed by the intractable opposition of France's president,

Charles De Gaulle. De Gaulle, for all his wartime links with Britain (or because of them), regarded the British as unreliable partners, and (if admitted to the Common Market) a potential threat to French leadership of the fledgling European union. He was even more suspicious of the United States, and had pursued an independent path since pulling France out of the North Atlantic Treaty Organization (NATO) in 1966. De Gaulle was not ready to admit the British to the organisation where France had primacy.

The year 1968 was an important one for the Common Market nations: France, West Germany, Italy, Belgium, Holland and Luxembourg. They took an important step towards closer trade integration by establishing a customs union, abolishing all import tariffs between them, and harmonising tariffs on goods imported from outside. Britain watched from the sidelines, a frustrated spectator. France still played a dominant role in the Common Market; West Germany was a growing industrial and financial powerhouse, but did not yet assert equal diplomatic muscle.

In Britain, government policy centred on correcting the balance of payments deficit; there would need to be defence cuts, and NHS prescription charges were reintroduced. The commitment to raising the school-leaving age, from 15 to 16, had to be postponed, and from September 1968 secondary school pupils would no longer enjoy free milk in the mid-morning break. Hardly surprising then that Labour was behind in the polls and losing by-elections at Dudley, Oldham West and Nelson & Colne. The Conservatives enjoyed an opinion-poll lead of about 20 per cent, Labour councillors were turfed out in the May local government elections and mutterings grew in Westminster corridors. To add to the angst, the Scottish Nationalists were becoming uppity, following Winnie Ewing's by-election win at Hamilton in 1967, and were encouraged when Conservatives at their party conference offered a Scottish Assembly. There were disturbing reports of political troubles brewing in Northern Ireland, where later in the year (August and October) civil rights marches took place, and – in Londonderry – sparked violence.

Harold Wilson remained outwardly imperturbable. He carried on, and if that meant pretending to be a Bruce Forsyth fan in 1968 – just as he had been a Beatles fan in 1965 and a World Cup Willie fan in 1966 – so be it. Besides, not all of it was gloom; there were some green shoots of recovery, while the 'Backing Britain' rallying cry might make people feel more cheerful, thus spend more, and so give the economy a boost. In truth, the 'Backing Britain' campaign always had a hollow Tin Pan Alley ring, and its impact was muted; in retrospect it received a hardly more favourable response than had Wilson's 1965 decision to give the Beatles their MBEs (John Lennon's medal reportedly rested on top of his auntie's television).

Back in 1968, aunties, even grandmothers, might admit to liking the Beatles – though an overt fondness for the Rolling Stones might seem a step too far. There was too much sex about, many people agreed, and there was much tut-tutting about all that drug taking encouraged by pop stars. The moral climate had not changed completely, however: a minor row at Edinburgh University caused the satirical journalist Malcolm Muggeridge to resign as rector over what he felt was a moral issue, when the university offered contraceptive pills free to students. That was taking 'Backing Britain' too far.

Trouble finding second gear?

In January 1968, following a change in divorce law, the irretrievable breakdown of a marriage became sufficient grounds for divorce. Disregarding any pessimistic symbolism, the government hailed a new industrial marriage between two big players in the British car industry. British Motor Holdings, still commonly known as British Motor Corporation (BMC), would merge with Leyland Motors to form British Leyland (BL). After a bright start, BL was destined for a turbulent history.

BMC had itself been the offspring of a commercial splicing, brought about in 1952 by the amalgamation of Austin and Morris, two founding names of British car-making, and incorporating other famous marques such as MG, Riley and Wolseley. In the early 1960s the outlook had been rosy with the success of the 1960s' iconic car, the Mini, designed by Alec Issigonis. Despite the Mini's captivating appeal, BMC was by 1968 struggling to retain market share and profitability; it simply had too many marques (Austin Mini, Morris Mini-Minor, Riley Elf, Wolseley Hornet …) competing for the same mini-market. The 1966 acquisition of Jaguar had added to the company's problems.

The 1968 merger was the brainchild of the Labour Government, and particularly of technology minister Tony Benn, who chaired the Industrial Reorganisation Committee. Led by Donald (later Lord) Stokes, Leyland Motor

Corporation (LMC) had a good track record in making commercial vehicles, owned known brands such as Rover, and was thought to have a more hard-nosed, realistic management. Stokes duly became boss of the new conglomerate.

Despite being Britain's largest car manufacturer by volume, with 40 per cent of sales, British Leyland was encumbered by an oversized, outdated model list. The days of the old Morris Oxford and Austin Cambridge models were numbered, and the popular 1100/1300 range was also showing its age by 1968, though still one of Britain's best-selling cars. Competition was largely US-backed: Ford (American-owned) and Rootes, recently acquired by Chrysler. Most people still thought British factories made decent enough cars – after all a Hillman Hunter (Rootes) won the 1968 London to Sydney Marathon, and a Hillman Imp won the RAC British Rally Championship. Also, Ford had a new model that looked promising, the Escort, to run alongside the Cortina and Corsair, and was also about to launch the Capri.

British car salesmen could tell themselves, truthfully, that most customers still bought British. Cheap foreign imports were practically non-existent, and foreign-made cars were generally held to be expensive, luxury items. The Japanese had, however, begun to spy out the UK market; the Daihatsu Compagno, today almost forgotten, had been a trailblazer in 1965, and in 1968 the Nissan Datsun brand made its UK debut. But for most buyers, British was still best on the local forecourt, and the desire to own a car was insatiable. A Triumph 1300 cost under £1,000, about the same as a teacher's starting annual salary; but it came with refinements – adjustable seats, a boot light, air-flow heating and ventilation. Car radios were still usually extras. Satnav, of course, was a fantasy notion – drivers used maps, even to check where the services were on the newest stretch of motorway. The M1 had just been extended to Leeds, and a further section of the M8 in Scotland was opened during the year.

BL seemed, briefly, to offer promise of a new industrial strategy for the 1970s: the new corporation combined car-making with buses, trucks, components manufacturers, construction machinery and metal casting. The seven divisions of the new conglomerate incorporated some 100 companies, and at its peak BLMC owned more than thirty-five manufacturing plants. The merger plastered over deep-seated industrial relations ailments, some of which today seem astonishingly parochial (for example, Austin workers were reluctant to work on Morris cars), and the two 'badges' remained competitive though now part of the same company (there were Minis bearing both badges). It was a thorough muddle, and the proliferation of assembly plants and supply chains inevitably meant increased costs, with too many models chasing the same buyers and too few outstanding export models to achieve volume-sales success.

Faced with its ageing backlist and strong competition, British Leyland needed new models for the 1970s: this need produced the Morris Marina and Austin Allegro, cars that, while selling reasonably well, did little to enhance their manufacturer's reputation. The five-door Maxi (1969) was the last BMC design from Issigonis, more innovative and 'Continental', but despite this, the British Leyland name never really caught on with the public, either in the UK or abroad. Hit by appalling industrial unrest, BL was partly nationalised in the 1970s, before being reorganised; today the BMW-owned Mini, Indian-owned Jaguar Land Rover, and US-owned Leyland Trucks are heirs to this troubled automotive kingdom.

While BL was eased into the world, Ford was at the Brussels Motor Show launching its new Escort. Brought in to replace the popular Anglia, the Escort was built at Ford's Hailwood plant in Merseyside. Its 1968 launch heralded a success story, with 2 million cars manufactured in the first six years. The Escort's styling was 1960s conventional but with innovative touches, notably the 'coke bottle' indented waistline and 'dog bone' radiator grille. An estate version arrived in March 1968. The original January models were two-door, but a four-door version went on sale the following year. Although the original Escorts had modest capacity engines (1100cc and 1300cc), the car's performance was sufficiently sporty to appeal, especially to the young – an appeal enhanced by the sports success of the twin-cam rally Escort which won the 1968 Saloon Car Championship. Escorts went on to become among the most successful rally cars in autosport history, and five succeeding generations took the Ford's modest supercar into the twenty-first century.

East is East and ...

Post Brexit referendum, the discussions in 1968 of 'Britain's place in the world' seem both other-worldly and yet curiously familiar. Was the country's destiny linked to that of its European neighbours? Or was its future bound to far-flung links, now largely post-imperial, with countries beyond Europe's shores? Europe in 1968 was starkly reflective of the post-war settlement; the Cold War was still icy, the Iron Curtain still in place, the Berlin Wall a brutal symbol of division. Events in Czechoslovakia in 1968 were to reinforce Western nervousness about the Soviet iron fist that still retained its grip on the satellite countries of the Warsaw Pact.

Prime Minister Wilson had stated (December 1964) that the country could not afford to give up its world role, but this was hot air. Defence Secretary Denis Healey had made it clear: Britain would withdraw from operations east of Suez, and in January 1968 the prime minister confirmed that the cutback was being brought forward, to save money. The new priority was European defence and the 'central front' – the defence of West Germany from Soviet aggression. The army and RAF would no longer keep such large forces overseas, since the escalation of tactical nuclear arsenals (and Soviet tank forces) required capable (and expensive) conventional forces in Europe. The navy might have to reconsider the role of its two remaining Second World War-vintage aircraft carriers (plans for three modern replacements having been cancelled in 1966). For modern strategists, this makes an interesting comparison with the UK's situation following the 2010 Strategic Defence Review, which reaffirmed the decision to build two new carriers, both bigger than the 1960s variety.

Where once British defence planners had their eyes on colonial maps and wide blue oceans, now Europe was the concern. Europe meant operating under the NATO umbrella, free of colonial responsibilities, and with the prospect of closer relations with both Western European allies and the United States. The lure of Europe was the song of the sirens on the rocks. There was a general feeling in Britain that somehow Europe was doing better than we were. Since the Treaty of Rome (1958) Community wages had outstripped prices, so the six members of the Common Market looked more prosperous. European cities rebuilt after the war were modern looking, visitors to the Continent no longer returned with horror stories about hotel plumbing, the railways seemed to work better than ours – and Germany had always had Europe's best roads.

The Macmillan government had begun the wooing of De Gaulle, but if 'Supermac' hoped memories of the old wartime alliance would smooth the path towards a happy outcome, he was to be disappointed. De Gaulle was deeply suspicious of Britain, even though in the immediate post-war years Churchill (with whom De Gaulle, as leader of the Free French in exile during the war, had had a prickly relationship) had been a Euro-enthusiast. Churchill had envisioned a unified Europe as an economic bulwark against Soviet expansionism, and the idea of unity out of conflict appealed to his sense of history. The British people were less romantic. Euro idealists hoped for a Europe of collaborating liberal democracies, a counterweight to the United States and USSR. Others saw the whole Euro plan as a birthday party for bureaucrats, and yet more felt they could not abandon historic ties of Empire. How could Britain turn its back on what had been the Empire, our kith and kin?

De Gaulle had militant opinions about most things, but especially about defence. France would not readily abandon its colonial past – and the scars from the war in Algeria (ended only in 1962) were still raw. De Gaulle was building up French forces, not scaling them back. His hostility to British membership of the EEC was fuelled by history, and by his paranoia concerning Britain's 'special relationship' with the United States.

That relationship, always unequal, was by the 1960s far less intimate. Old wartime colleagues (if not always friends) had left the scene, and there was a stark disparity in 'hard power' between the two countries. The elder statesman Macmillan had struck up a relationship with President Kennedy, but Wilson felt no comparable warmth from Johnson, the tall Texan now in the White House. The prime minister and the president talked, about Vietnam and other issues, but Britain's refusal to take part in the Vietnam War had strained the old alliance. The United States was the superpower: only the USSR came close to matching it militarily. The Russians could amass vast land forces, with tanks and missiles, and they had terrifying numbers of intercontinental missiles, heavy bombers and nuclear submarines, but the Soviet Navy had no aircraft carriers, no oceanic fleets to rival the global reach of the US Navy.

Nor had Britain, not any more. The rundown after the Second World War and the Korean War in the early 1950s had seriously reduced the Royal Navy's strength, although some admirals might retain pretensions to old glories and, with the forthcoming acquisition of Britain's nuclear deterrent, scented a new role. The Royal Navy had long been accustomed to sailing the world's oceans: showing the flag, protecting British interests, and keeping the peace by force if necessary. To sustain such global reach in the 1960s would have been a daunting challenge, even for an economy more robust and a government less inclined to consign the anachronisms of Empire to history. Nevertheless, the Royal Navy still regarded itself as a world navy. It might no longer have battleships, and its surviving big fleet carriers were under threat, yet the navy still saw its main concerns as oceanic trade, colonial outposts, and defence arteries from Suez and beyond to the Gulf, the Indian Ocean, Singapore and Hong Kong. Few in the Admiralty were ready to see Her Majesty's ships relegated solely to hunting Soviet submarines, or (even worse) operating fishery protection and border patrols in home waters. 'Join the navy and see the world' was still a recruitment incentive, as it was for Britain's army and air force. The harsh reality was that there would be less of the world to see in future, at least from the deck of a ship flying the White Ensign.

Labour, never comfortable with imperial and colonial roles, decided that for the next decade Britain's efforts should be concentrated on, or even confined to, the European theatre, and the NATO strategy of containing any Soviet threat on the Continent. This meant reductions in the activities and location of military units, including naval ships and overseas air force commitments, retaining token forces only in Singapore, Brunei, Bahrain and Hong Kong. The Far East Air Force, equipped with Canberras, Hunters, Lightnings and Shackletons, would be disbanded from 1971. The future of the navy's two big aircraft carriers was subject to review. *Ark Royal* was being refitted to operate US Phantom jets; the other carrier, HMS *Eagle*, had just emerged from a refit without such modification – so its long-term usefulness was in doubt. In the Commons, the navy minister (David Owen, future foreign secretary) denied rumours that both ships were to be handed over to NATO and re-equipped with American aircraft. In the event, both would be scrapped in the next decade; of the remaining smaller carriers, *Centaur* and *Albion* were scrapped in 1973, *Bulwark* in 1984, and *Hermes* was sold to India in 1986. The navy was offered replacements: ships originally described as 'through-deck cruisers', but which eventually materialised as the Invincible-class 'ski-jump' carriers operating Harriers.

The admirals battled with the bureaucrats to plead for new, if smaller, warships with gas turbine propulsion, such as the Type 42 destroyer HMS *Sheffield* then on order (and sunk in the Falklands War of 1982). Most of the navy's ships would be destroyers or frigates; its elderly cruisers, requiring costly refits, did not serve long in the fleet: *Lion* went to the scrapyard in 1975, *Blake* in 1982, with *Tiger* last to go in 1986. Manpower was to be cut to 79,000 by 1973, though the closure of overseas fuel depots called for an increase in the Royal Fleet Auxiliary's tanker strength, in case of future far-flung operations or 'showing the flag'. Despite the rundown, the Royal Navy was still a force to be reckoned with. Some fifty ships (around a quarter of the fleet strength) gathered for the Fleet Review at Rosyth in August, led by HMS *Bulwark*.

Denis Healey, defence minister, agreed that the armed services had reason to feel upset, as they suffered these changes. The RAF's fifty-two squadrons would fall to thirty-eight over the next ten years; the air marshals were already concerned at the obsolescence of their aircraft. The army, smarting under regimental reorganisations, did slightly better, losing only four of its twenty-three armoured regiments in the next decade. The defence cuts removed two organisations responsible for sterling service during and after the Second World War: the Civil Defence Corps and the Auxiliary Fire Service, both disbanded. Defence spending as a percentage of overall government expenditure was just over 13 per cent (down from about 18 per cent a decade earlier). Manpower stood at around 395,000 personnel, still almost double the number today (just under 200,000 in 2016).

The defence cuts were a clear sign of changing priorities and shifts in alignment. No longer was Britain to play a leading role 'east of Suez' – a retreat inevitable ever since the Suez Canal operations of 1956 had revealed Britain's relative weakness when faced with US (and UN) opposition to an independent projection of force in support of policy. An interesting historical footnote to the defence debate was that 1968 proved to be the first year in the twentieth century in which no serving British soldier had been killed in action.

The US Government was unhappy about Britain's withdrawal east of Suez. President Johnson expressed dismay, as did the secretary of state, Dean Rusk. But the pull-back of its supposed closest ally from the Indian Ocean offered an opportunity too, and Britain's desire to buy US weapons, such as Polaris, gave the Americans a bargaining chip. An Indian Ocean base for the US had obvious advantages, and who better to provide one than the old colonial master? The US Government spotted a suitable site – the Indian Ocean island territory of Diego Garcia, British since the early 1800s and part of the British Indian Ocean Territory. True, some people lived there: about 1,000 islanders known as Chagossians. But they could be relocated. The Chagos Islanders had to go, and they were removed between 1968 and 1973 so that the United States could construct a military base on their island. Some came to the UK, a number settling in Crawley, and a long legal row over their plight, and possible return, rumbled on for decades (and is still rumbling). In the meantime, Diego Garcia became an important US military base and staging point, with runways for large aircraft, port anchorages and refuelling facilities.

As Britain started to withdraw, US diplomats took a keener interest in the Gulf states, whose rulers were nervous at the prospect of losing the protection of a British military presence. The Middle East was a simmering flashpoint, following Israel's victory over Arab armies in the Six Day War (1967), though the regime in Iran (under the shah) seemed stable. In Iraq there was yet another revolution in 1968, when the Ba'ath Party leader Ahmed Hasan al-Bakr overthrew the Arif regime. Among al-Bakr's supporters was an as yet obscure army officer named Saddam Hussein.

2

February

MEDITATION MATTERS

The not so magical meditation tour

On 15 February 1968, John Lennon flew to India. He was followed days later by the other Beatles and friends to spend several weeks of transcendental meditation with the Maharishi Mahesh Yogi. The Maharishi was then 41 or so, and had become known from his TV appearances as the 'giggling guru'. The idea of a guru, or teacher, who could induct Westerners into the higher planes of Eastern mysticism had seemingly great appeal, especially among the top pop elite.

The Maharishi had gained minor celebrity in the late 1950s, touring the world to teach transcendental meditation, but his fame really blossomed after he caught the attention of George Harrison of the Beatles. All four members of the premier pop group attended a lecture the Indian 'mystic' gave in London in August 1967. They subsequently went to hear him again in Wales – a trip to Bangor that also included Mick Jagger, Marianne Faithfull and Cilla Black, among others. The suggestion that visitors donate a week's pay to the Maharishi caused only a slight flicker of hesitation.

A trip to India, considered in 1967, had to be postponed following the death in August that year of the Beatles' manager, Brian Epstein. In 1968, the trip was restored to the itinerary, perhaps to help ease the sadness and the gap left by Epstein's passing. It was intended as a peaceful interlude away from the mayhem of Beatlemania, though John Lennon's domestic peace, and marriage, were both being disturbed by almost daily telegrams from Yoko Ono, a Japanese artist who had become besotted with him.

The Beatles' visit to India attracted widespread media interest. They travelled to Rishikesh, where, in the foothills of the Himalayas, Maharishi Mahesh Yogi held instruction sessions. The entourage included wives (Cynthia Lennon, Maureen Starkey, Patti Boyd), girlfriends (Jane Asher), a Beach Boy (Mike Love) and folk singer Donovan. Mia Farrow, star of one of the hit films of the year, *Rosemary's Baby*, also came calling at the Maharishi's ashram.

Their time at Rishikesh, 'yoga capital of the world', or what Ringo Starr called a kind of 'spiritual Butlin's', involved an austere life in contrast to the pop stars' normal hectic routine. They ate communal meals (vegetarian), and eschewed alcohol on the Maharishi's advice – though booze was smuggled in surreptitiously by a Beatles aide. By day they sat in sessions for meditation and to hear lectures from the Maharishi, who liked to address followers from a dais laden with flowers. When not meditating, they made music, or art, or conversation; it was all very relaxing. An on-site Indian tailor was available to make Indian-style clothes for the Western visitors, and before leaving they all posed for a group photo, adorned with floral garlands.

First to fly home were Ringo and wife Maureen, who left on 4 March, soon followed by Paul McCartney, who had business in London, and Jane Asher. John Lennon and George Harrison stayed the longest, for seven weeks – a reasonable time to meditate – though their departure was blemished by obscure press rumours of disagreements about money and 'inappropriate behaviour' by the Maharishi (Mia Farrow allegedly recalled the guru trying to put his arm around her). By the end of June, all the Beatles were back in Britain, but the Maharishi had some priceless publicity.

By the time the meditation was over – he called it 'a nice holiday' – John Lennon was more concerned with thoughts of Yoko Ono, and with the dissolving state of his marriage to Cynthia. In October 1968, following a police raid, Lennon and Ono were charged with possession of cannabis. After India, Cynthia had subsequently gone on holiday to Greece, arriving home in May, earlier than expected, to find Lennon and Ono together. The couple's marriage was legally ended on 8 November 1968.

The Beatles had stopped touring in 1966, to concentrate on album work, and on individual projects such as George Harrison's first solo album, which featured Indian musicians. The visit to India was in fact the last time the Beatles travelled abroad together as the world's most famous foursome. Afterwards they said the Maharishi had been very kind. But the world assumed the experience to have been less than what was promised or expected.

They were, as one of the Beatles said later, very young back then. The Maharishi continued teaching, and trying to change human history (his stated hope), until his death in 2008.

On and off the box

Television-watching in 1968 often required serial commitment. Just three channels, no recording, no catch-up. Viewers and programme-schedulers liked to know what was coming up – same time, each week. The end of a long-running series often left a gap; in February 1968 *The Prisoner* ended its run, its enigmatic storyline having made a cult series. *The Prisoner*'s star, Patrick McGoohan, was one of the biggest names in 1960s TV, having become a star through *Danger Man*, as the eponymous special agent hero.

Other family favourites faded from British screens. ITV decided that two of its original quiz shows had run their course and scrapped *Take Your Pick*, presented by Michael Miles, who whipped up audience participation by challenging contestants to 'open the box' (and see what prize, if any, they had won) rather than accept the cash he waved in front of them. Also axed was *Double Your Money*, another show dating from the beginning of commercial television in Britain, compèred by Hughie Greene who grinned to camera while quizzing contestants. Hughie Greene remained a frequent presence on the box with his talent show *Opportunity Knocks*, the 1968 forerunner of shows such as *The X-Factor*, and on which Mary Hopkin performed in May.

Fans of Scottish dancing and Caledonian music in general were left bereft by the removal of *White Heather Club*, a series that had run since 1958 and which brought to audiences inside and outside Scotland the talents of people such as Jimmy Shand, Jimmy Logan, Andy Stewart, Kenneth McKellar and Moira Anderson, and the singing duo Robin Hall and Jimmy McGregor. Unashamedly 'tartan' (the men usually wore kilts), the show has a particular place in British TV history, but would now appear almost as eccentric as the Black and White Minstrels. This singing and dancing entertainment show, hugely popular at the time, is now regarded by some as extremely embarrassing, if not offensive, because it involved the traditional minstrel 'blacking up' (the show ran on BBC1 until 1978).

Other changes to programming in 1968 affected children's television. Exiting stage left were Captain Scarlet and the Mysterons, and the singing piglets Pinky and Perky. New shows airing for the first time included *Magpie*, an ITV rival to the BBC's *Blue Peter*, which ran until 1980. For the slightly more adult there were new situation comedies: *Father, Dear Father*, with Patrick Cargill, and *Please Sir*, with John Alderton in the classroom. And there was football. Commercial TV bosses decided that the BBC had hogged the soccer field to itself for too long, having started *Match of the Day* back in 1964. In competition, they launched *The Big Match*, at first screened by London Weekend on Sunday afternoons. *The Big Match* presenters were Brian Moore and analyst Jimmy Hill, moving into television after his varied career first as a player with Fulham, then as chairman of the players' union, the PFA, and manager of Coventry City, where he lifted the club from relative obscurity to the First Division.

The BBC also found itself with a winner, though without at first recognising the fact. Jimmy Perry and David Croft's idea for a comedy series about a Home Guard unit during the Second World War had struck some at the BBC as eccentrically ill-advised. Was the war a suitable subject for family comedy? Would the British find war stories funny, and if so, wouldn't the prospective audience be middle-aged? Would they be upset at the war effort being ridiculed? Surely young people would not watch a series about the mishaps of part-time soldiers? Anyway, *The Army Game* had 'done' the army before on TV; surely once was enough. But Perry and Croft persisted, and on 31 July 1968 the first episode of *Dad's Army* ('The Man and the Hour') was aired, introducing the seven principal platoon members who were to popularise the show for the next nine years. The series is, of course, still showing.

Classics were always well done on television although, naturally, best on the 'serious' channel! Eric Porter gained a BAFTA for his performance as Soames in *The Forsyte Saga*. The 1967 adaptation of John Galsworthy's novels proved so successful when screened on BBC2 that from September 1968, all twenty-six episodes were repeated, to reach the much larger audience on BBC1. The serial became a 'Sunday night stay-in', with audiences peaking to 18 million for the final episode.

Those were indeed the days of mass audiences. With only two channels having nationwide coverage (BBC2 was available only to a minority of viewers) 'watching television' meant everyone in the family looking at the same thing at the same time. To have more than one TV set at home would have been considered super-extravagant by most. The TV usually sat in the sitting room, or wherever the warmest fire was, so everyone could gather to watch the most popular shows, be it *Top of the Pops*, *Dixon of Dock Green*, *Doctor Who*, *The Forsyte Saga* – or even (for the highbrow) *University Challenge*, hosted in 1968 by Bamber Gascoigne and on ITV.

The year 1968 was also notable for the first BBC broadcast of the Eurovision Song Contest in colour. The song contest was held in London on 6 April at the Royal Albert Hall, and several European countries took the transmission in colour. The only British channel as yet broadcasting in colour was BBC2, and a song contest, even under the Eurovision banner, was regarded by BBC management as not really the kind of programming suited to its ever-so-slightly snootily earnest second channel. So BBC1 screened the show live in monochrome, with BBC2 broadcasting a colour repeat next day. Cliff Richard, with the British entry 'Congratulations', was the pre-show favourite to win, but the result was to prove all too familiar in subsequent contests. The song, a big hit for Cliff, failed (just) to win over the Eurovision juries, finishing second to a Spanish entry catchily titled 'La La La' and sung by Massiel, whose real name was Maria de los Ángeles Felisa Santamaría Espinosa.

It was a year of franchise change in the independent networks, with the new contract round resulting in several changes. ABC lost its weekend franchise in the North and Midlands, and Granada and ATV extended their North and Midlands coverage to seven days. In the capital, London Weekend (LWT) replaced ATV London and Rediffusion London from Friday night to Sunday. LWT had been set up by a consortium that included David Frost, whose fame was such that he had been signed to present three shows a week on American television.

LWT's debut in July was disrupted by a technicians' strike, which spread to other networks and caused a two-week period of emergency scheduling put out by management. Having weathered that, LWT registered disappointing ratings, blamed on a Saturday night judged by some critics as too upmarket (too much Stravinsky, no Val Doonican). The London weekday franchise passed from Rediffusion to Thames Television, which saw an opening for Sunday football on the box and launched *The Big Match*.

Staying in was becoming a habit. This meant tough times for the cinema, as families stayed at home to watch *Coronation Street*, or the sixth series of *The Avengers*, which in 1968 saw Linda Thorson's Tara King replace Diana Rigg's Emma Peel. From a staggering 1.5 billion cinema admissions in 1948, the number of people going to the pictures had shrunk to 754 million in 1958, and by 1968 had dwindled again to 237 million. The decline yet had some way to go (admissions are today currently around the 170 million mark), and in fact 1968 was a good year for films. A night at the cinema whisked picturegoers away from anxieties about Britain's role in the world, student rebellion, Soviet obduracy, and why Britain had not won the Eurovision Song

Contest. There were plenty of escapist films – none more so than Stanley Kubrick's *2001: A Space Odyssey*. This was mind-blowing, visually stunning, and with a soundtrack that mixed the music of Richard and Johann Strauss, as 'Also Sprach Zarathrustra' and 'The Blue Danube' waltz transported audiences from a prehistoric Earth to the Moon and beyond.

For the first year since 1948 there was no British Academy Film Award for Best British Film. The category was discontinued, returning in 1992. But there were good films to be seen, with established stars and a crop of promising newcomers. In 1968 Spencer Tracy received a BAFTA Best Actor Award for *Guess Who's Coming to Dinner?*, ahead of British talent which included Trevor Howard (*The Charge of the Light Brigade*), Ron Moody (*Oliver!*) and Nicol Williamson *(The Bofors Gun)*. Katherine Hepburn won plaudits for her performance alongside Tracy, and for her role as Eleanor of Aquitaine in *The Lion in Winter* (with Peter O'Toole). 'Most Promising Newcomer' was Dustin Hoffman, for *The Graduate*, in which he played Benjamin Braddock to Anne Bancroft's seductive Mrs Robinson.

Cinemagoers could also enjoy the novelty of Sean Connery in a western with Brigitte Bardot (*Shalako*), Dick van Dyke driving a flying car (*Chitty Chitty Bang Bang*) and Richard Burton starring alongside Clint Eastwood in the Second World War thriller *Where Eagles Dare*, using the now immortal radio call sign 'Broadsword calling Danny Boy'. In an age of film-making before CGI and featuring astonishing/unbelievable sequences of action so fast they almost defy comprehension, many films of 1968 still give pleasure. For those retaining any thought to be provoked after watching *2001*, there was *Up the Junction* (with a youthful Denis Waterman and Maureen Lipman) and Lindsay Anderson's *If*, about violent revolt in an English public school, which had an X-certificate slapped on it before release in December 1968. A surrealist mixture of satire and fantasy, the film was seen as a scathing critique of society, but it also attracted criticism for what some saw as its ambivalence towards the use of violence. The year's most successful movie was probably *Oliver!*, the screen version of Lionel Bart's musical, featuring Ron Moody as Fagin, plus Mark Lester as Oliver Twist and Jack Wilde as the Artful Dodger. There was also the first instalment of what was to become a long-running franchise, *Planet of the Apes*.

Actor Sir Donald Wolfit had a relatively small part in *The Charge of the Light Brigade*; it was his last film role, for he died on 7 February 1968, remembered as perhaps the last in a line of Victorian-style actor-managers, touring the country with 'classics' in which he played the leading roles. Wolfit had earned his knighthood over many hours and miles of touring; he had often seemed an outsider, a throwback to an earlier era of melodrama, to actors who preferred the booming voice and grand gesture to the subtler arts demanded by modern drama teachers and the film and television cameras. Britain's most eminent theatrical knights were a celebrated trio: Laurence Olivier, John Gielgud and Ralph Richardson, colleagues and collaborators over many years, and by 1968 regarded as national treasures. Donald Wolfit, meanwhile, had continued taking classics to the masses – an increasingly unrewarding mission when theatres in provincial cities were either closing altogether or being converted into bingo halls.

Wolfit started his own touring company in 1937, after a brief spell at the Shakespeare Memorial Theatre, whose management refused to finance a provincial tour. As lead, he had starred in London productions of *King Lear* and *Richard II*, and during the war he and his company had performed abridged adaptations of Shakespeare in London for lunchtime audiences. The playwright Ronald Harwood worked for a time as Wolfit's dresser, and his play *The Dresser* (1980) features, in 'Sir', just such a Shakespearean actor-manager in wartime Britain, struggling with his own fallibilities as well as the exigencies of putting on plays when bombs were falling and actors were in short supply. Wolfit was probably best known for his ego, and lack of humility; it was often said that he considered himself the greatest actor in the world, but his energy and his commitment to the theatre in a career lasting from 1920 to 1968 earned him warm tributes in the obituary columns.

At a time of 'liberation' from what many saw as restrictive conventions in the theatre and cinema, there was a major change in the law, with the abolition of the Lord Chamberlain's power to pre-censor any play deemed likely to shock, offend or degrade. Similar censorship had been around since Shakespeare's day, but the pre-1968 rules had been in place since 1843, banning obscenity, stage nudity (unless static), blasphemy and anything else that might offend. The 1968 Theatres Act removed from the Lord Chamberlain's office the power to refuse a theatre licence to any play judged to offend public morality, although theatre managements could still be liable to prosecution for obscenity.

Stage nudity, previously mostly confined to the Windmill Theatre in London and rundown provincial theatres trying to fill seats with striptease, was suddenly in the box office, with the arrival in London of the new American musical *Hair*. A hit both on Broadway and now in London, the show made liberal use of four-letter words and its cast stripped naked on stage. The abolition of the Lord Chamberlain's powers of theatre censorship did not (to the regret of some, no doubt) lead to an outbreak of lewdness, though in a production of *Dr Faustus* at Stratford-upon-Avon, Helen of Troy appeared naked. The Royal Shakespeare Company had a new artistic director in 28-year-old Trevor Nunn, replacing Peter Hall, who left after ten years in charge.

Rolf Hochhuth's *Soldiers*, a controversial play about the Second World War and in particular Poland, Allied bombing and Winston Churchill, finally had a London production. Laurence Olivier and Kenneth Tynan had tried to stage the play the previous year at the National Theatre, which was still at the Old Vic while awaiting its new home on the South Bank. Although this move was confirmed during the year, the new National Theatre complex would not open officially until 1977. *Soldiers* had been rejected by the National Theatre's board, which included Lord Chandos, a wartime colleague of Churchill, but in 1968 the play was put on at the New Theatre, after cuts.

Royal family revealed

In February 1968, Queen Elizabeth II marked the sixteenth year of her accession to the throne. While the world worried about Vietnam, Czechoslovakia and student unrest, the advisers to the royal family suggested it was time the palace opened its doors, metaphorically speaking, to allow the public a more intimate view of life inside 'the firm', as senior members called it. In the early years of the Queen's reign, the mystique of the royal family had been preserved by traditional protocol, though relaxed to allow press and television coverage of the Queen's activities in what had been, briefly, hailed by some in the media as the 'new Elizabethan Age'.

In 1968 came the suggestion for a documentary film, to show the Queen, Prince Philip and their children as informally as possible. The idea was put forward by the film-producer Lord Brabourne, son-in-law of Lord Louis Mountbatten. Mountbatten had been fully aware of the power of the press throughout his career, in the military during the Second World War and as Britain's last viceroy in India. It was time, the film's supporters suggested, to show the royal family in a contemporary way, more in tune with the 1960s.

The proposal was accepted; filming took place during 1968, and the programme was shown in 1969. It would slot in neatly with publicity around the investiture of Prince Charles as Prince of Wales, scheduled for 1969, the year of his 21st birthday. This ceremony at Caernarfon Castle would inevitably be a possibly awkward conjunction of medieval and modern, so a film showing the Prince and other members of the family doing what ordinary people did – having picnics, decorating the Christmas tree, taking the dogs for a walk, watching television – would be a useful counterpoint. The documentary was directed by Richard Cawston, with a script commentary by Antony Jay and voiced by Michael Flanders (of Flanders and Swann).

The Queen's 1968 programme of overseas tours was comparatively light. Her major official visits took her to Brazil and Chile in November, and among the presents she was given were a pair of sloths from the Brazilian rainforest. Prince Charles had begun the year as a student at Trinity College, Cambridge, studying archaeology and anthropology; his exam results, made public in June, showed he had performed creditably, but he decided to switch to history as his main subject. The plan was to send him to Wales, to the University College at Aberystwyth, in the spring of 1969, to study Welsh language and culture, and prepare for the investiture on 1 July 1969 – a dressing-up occasion to give any young man nightmares, especially when the ritual was to be performed by his mother. To emphasise that he was a thoroughly modern monarch-to-be, Charles was also pictured taking flying lessons in an RAF Chipmunk at Tangmere.

Charles's sister Princess Anne, now 18, was about to leave Benenden School, which had been visited by her mother during the year. The junior princes Andrew (8) and Edward (6) were at school, and in the filming, the Queen was persuaded to allow herself to be shown buying sweets for Edward, while the Duke of Edinburgh showed them how to cook sausages during a family barbecue. Later, opinions within the family, and outside, about the value of the programme were divided. The public seemed to like it – *The Royal Family* was screened in 1969 on both the BBC and ITV, and positive responses included viewers' comments that it had made the Queen seem more approachable, 'just like us'. Her Majesty was perhaps less sure about letting in the cameras. After its initial transmission, the full programme has never been shown again.

The Queen's round of official engagements in 1968 included the usual eclectic mix: opening the new Royal Mint at Llantrisant in Wales; reopening the rebuilt Euston Station; a cinema visit to watch Franco Zeffirelli's film of *Romeo and Juliet*. The Queen Mother led the royal party to November's Royal Variety Performance at the London Palladium, along with Princess Margaret and her husband Lord Snowdon, Prince Charles and Princess Anne. It was regarded as one of the best shows yet: the line-up featured Frankie Howerd, Mike Yarwood, Ted Rogers, Sacha Distel, Engelbert Humperdinck, Val Doonican, Petula Clark, Arthur Askey, Aimi Macdonald and Lionel Blair, plus Motown superstars Diana Ross and the Supremes. In charge of proceedings was Des O'Connor, spared his usual ribbing from Morecambe and Wise because the comedy duo had to pull out owing to illness.

The royal family lost a prominent and much-loved member in 1968: Princess Marina, Duchess of Kent, a first cousin of the Duke of Edinburgh. Their fathers were brothers, and Marina had married the Queen's uncle, the Duke of Kent, youngest of the four sons of King George V. George, Duke of Kent, had a stylish, if raffish, reputation, and was a popular member of the royal family until his death in a wartime air crash in 1942. In carrying out official engagements at home and abroad, Princess Marina had been admired for her charm and style, featuring frequently in national and international 'best dressed' lists. She had been a familiar face at the Wimbledon tennis championships, where she had for many years presented the winners' trophies, and was also chancellor of the new University of Kent (1963). Soon after the announcement that the duchess was suffering from a brain tumour, she died at Kensington Palace on 27 August 1968, at the age of 61. On 29 August, two days before the duchess' funeral, her husband's remains, previously interred at St George's Chapel, Windsor, were moved to the Royal Burial Ground at Frogmore, where the two were laid to rest together. Princess Marina's funeral was attended by her brother-in-law, the Duke of Windsor (the former King Edward VIII). The occasion would prove to be the last royal ceremony attended by the exiled duke in Britain before his death in 1972.

3

March

PREPARE FOR THE WORST …

LBJ's month to forget

President Lyndon Baines Johnson of the United States could be forgiven for not considering 1968 one of his better years. First there was the unfortunate affair of the USS *Pueblo* and the North Koreans. A week later, the war in Vietnam took a turn – for better or worse depended on which side you were on.

Vice president (and largely sidelined) under President John Kennedy, Johnson found himself thrust into the presidency after Kennedy's 1963 shooting in Dallas. He had then won a landslide victory in the 1964 presidential election, crushing his Republican opponent, Barry Goldwater. This enabled him to press ahead with liberal domestic measures including the 1964 Civil Rights Act and, in 1968, a further Civil Rights Act (mainly to do with ending discrimination in house sales or lets). Just when the civil rights situation seemed easier, the president had been sucked into the morass of an escalating Vietnam War, and by 1968 anti-war protests at home – especially among the young – were becoming ever more noisy, anguished and often violent. On top of these concerns, the president woke up one morning in January 1968 to be told that one of his warships had gone missing. The ship was the USS *Pueblo*, and it had been 'arrested' by North Korea.

On 23 January 1968 the *USS Pueblo* was off (or in) Korean waters; officially designated an environmental research vessel, its prime purpose was intelligence gathering. Tension was high on the Korean peninsula, following an incursion by North Korean troops into South Korea. The Americans later insisted the ship was in international waters; North Korea said it had strayed into its territory. The *Pueblo* was challenged by a North Korean warship, which fired warning shots, while North Korean MiGs flew overhead; then North Koreans opened fire with serious intent, killing one US crewman. All this time, the US military was aware of what was going on, but had no ships or aircraft close enough to intervene. The Pentagon could only watch and listen as the *Pueblo* was boarded and her crew arrested by the North Koreans.

The eighty-two US sailors spent the next eleven months as POWs in a North Korean prison, and the Americans afterwards claimed they were tortured physically and psychologically. Negotiations for their release dragged on all year, with the North Koreans demanding the US admit 'guilt' for the incursion into their territorial waters and apologise. Eventually, the two sides agreed on a form of words, and the sailors came home in December, but the North Koreans kept the *Pueblo*. The ship is still theirs, and still the subject of US demands for its return.

The *Pueblo*'s skipper, Commander Lloyd Bucher, came in for criticism; there were suggestions that he had too readily signed a 'confession' the day after his seizure, admitting that his ship had been spying. Bucher's actions were criticised by some as feeble and unmilitary, but praised by others on both wings of US politics. The Right blamed Washington for being faint-hearted in its anti-Communist policy, and saw no reason why the crew of a small, poorly equipped ship should have been expected to sacrifice themselves; the liberal left saw Bucher's action as rational and humane, doing his best to safeguard the welfare of his crew. Naval tradition, harsher critics pointed out, forbade any ship's captain from allowing his ship to be searched by a foreign state without consent, so long as it had the capacity to resist. Whether *Pueblo* had such capacity was open to question. A Senate Armed Services Committee was scathing about deficiencies in US military intelligence, and blamed the Pentagon for the whole disgrace.

It was not a good time for Pentagon top brass. In the Vietnam War, the enemy (North Vietnam and the Vietcong) showed no sign of giving up, or even giving ground, in the face of what on paper looked like overwhelming US superiority. It had been three years since the first US combat troops had begun to fight in South Vietnam in 1965; previous US involvement was restricted to 'military advisers' helping the South Vietnamese combat aggression from Communist North Vietnam and its allies, the Vietcong.

The US had a twofold strategy: bomb North Vietnam to reduce its capacity and will to wage war, and carry out 'search and destroy' missions in South Vietnam to defeat the Vietcong and pacify the countryside. Neither was having the desired effect. South Vietnam's generals were uncomfortable, and undemocratic allies and traditional friends (such as Britain) had declined to assist the Americans, though Australia had sent troops. At home, the war had split US public opinion between 'Doves', who called for US withdrawal and peace talks, and 'Hawks' who thought Johnson's policy too timidly gradualist, urging the US to use all its military muscle to crush the North and finish the war once and for all.

The rising cost of the Vietnam War in financial and human terms was threatening Johnson's domestic programme and his popularity. The rich objected to tax hikes, the poor protested because it seemed that they were bearing the brunt of the casualties (the better-off seemed better able to avoid the draft). Riots in cities (Chicago, Cleveland, Detroit, Los Angeles, New York) were sparked by a combination of anti-war protest and racial unrest. Johnson saw his personal poll ratings plummet, with the next presidential election due in November 1968. Once unassailable, the Texan now faced challengers within his own Democratic Party, the most high profile being Senator Eugene McCarthy (already gobbling up the anti-war votes) and Robert F. Kennedy (brother of JFK), both of whom announced their intention to challenge Johnson for the Democratic presidential nomination.

The Tet Offensive at the end of January 1968 piled more bad news into the president's in-tray. Nowhere in the Pentagon's script for winning the war was there a mention of a bunch of Vietcong guerrillas in South Vietnamese uniforms storming the US Embassy in Saigon, which is what happened early in the morning of 31 January. The Communists had selected the Tet holiday (the lunar new year), a traditional time for a truce in war, and a time when many Vietnamese families were on the roads, visiting relatives. Busy roads provided cover for Vietcong guerrilla movements. They launched a major offensive, of which the embassy attack was a part, during which North Vietnamese and Vietcong troops attacked key points such as Hue and Saigon, and other towns and military bases across South Vietnam.

For a short while there was near panic and confusion in South Vietnam, with alarm and dismay in Washington. The attacks soon ran out of steam, and the Communist forces were driven back by US and South Vietnamese forces, only to regroup and try again later in the year. Overall, Tet could be claimed by the Americans as a Communist defeat, since the objectives struck at were soon recaptured, but the psychological impact was profound, the Communists gaining far more than temporary possession of a few targets. Their temerity was in itself offensive, and shocking, shaking the confidence of Americans at home in their leaders. Vietnam was a TV war: each reverse, each small victory screened nightly. And now this. How could their boys be winning, Americans asked, when the country's embassy came under siege in the heart of Saigon? For South Vietnam's President Nguyễn Văn Thiệu to declare martial law seemed a further indication that years of US military effort, human losses and money had not achieved anything like victory. After Tet, even fewer Americans really believed their army was winning this war.

The Tet Offensive rumbled on through February until the last Communist units were pushed out of Hue Province. Washington claimed that the Communists had lost more than 33,000 combatants killed; Allied losses were over 3,000 – one-third of them American. US Commander William Westmoreland compared Tet to the 1944 Battle of the Bulge, insisting the Communists had suffered a defeat, albeit after a 'temporary psychological advantage'.

But that advantage was huge. The attacks revealed that the Americans and South Vietnamese had, in fact, a fragile hold upon a country through which the Communists were still able to move, assemble and attack seemingly at will. Television and press coverage of the Tet Offensive suggested confusion and chaos, not control, while horrific images such as a South Vietnamese police chief executing a Vietcong prisoner with a pistol shot to the head added fuel to the fires of protest.

Anti-war protests intensified. Ordinary Americans, and many others in friendly nations such as Britain, wondered: If, with half a million 'boots on the ground', the Americans could not win this war, then what was the point? Westmoreland asked for more troops. Johnson refused. Instead, the president ordered a reduction of US bombing of North Vietnam. Then on 31 March, Johnson made a dramatic announcement: he had decided against running again for president, but was withdrawing for the sake of national unity. He would not allow himself to be nominated. The US Government would explore ways to begin talks with the North Vietnam regime. There would be a new US president come what may; not LBJ, but McCarthy, Kennedy, Vice President Hubert Humphrey (now certain to seek the Democrats' nomination) or the Republican challenger, Richard Nixon.

Peace talks, at first tentative, began in Paris in May, at a time when a new wave of North Vietnam and Vietcong attacks began – a virtual second Tet – to be followed by more incursions in August. The US military insisted it needed more troops for an 'accelerated pacification programme', to achieve final victory through a combined US and South Vietnamese offensive. But the political will for such a move was gone; Johnson decided to limit US bombing raids on North Vietnam, and impose a ceiling on troop numbers in the South. By November the US had ceased all air attacks in North Vietnam. The peace talks that began with such hopes made slow progress, however, and the war dragged on for a further five years, into the Nixon presidency, before a cease-fire was signed in January 1973, after which US ground forces withdrew. By then the writing was on the wall. After two more years of war and retreat, in April 1975 the government of South Vietnam surrendered. North Vietnamese troops marched into Saigon, where the Tet Offensive had caused such shock and awe seven years before.

'The optimist with the raincoat'

This was Harold Wilson's description of himself, an optimist, but an optimist who carries a raincoat – in his case, the Gannex raincoat he frequently wore. That optimism was being sorely tested in 1968. Wilson celebrated his 52nd birthday on 11 March – still young enough to build on his reputation as an election winner and, as prime minister, match his earlier brilliance: the Huddersfield-born grammar school boy who had soared into and through Oxford, picked up a First on the way, and whose forte as a student athlete had been the quarter of a mile – the sustained, one-lap sprint. The former grammar school boy justified Labour's decision to abolish grammar schools by claiming every new comprehensive would be a grammar school for all.

Astute enough to know that Britain was at a turning point in its history, Wilson was perhaps less sure of which way it was to go. He was no great enthusiast for the Commonwealth, which was proving troublesomely critical of British policy towards Rhodesia and Nigeria, and (as always) South Africa. Wilson had been ready to make advances towards Europe, but once again perfidious Albion had been spurned by General De Gaulle, whose haughty profile cast a long shadow. Wilson was short of allies – friendly countries such as Ireland and Denmark were hopeful of joining the Common Market too, as were some Tories (Edward Heath for one), but his own Labour side in Westminster was ambivalent. Ideally, socialists favoured internationalism, planning and partnership; but the left had reservations about this new Europe, which might become a monolith of multinational capitalism. The trade unions were, on the whole, anti-Europe, even if some TUC members might envy the apparent power of French unions to block roads and bend governments to their will. Wilson thought the Americans might become even more important as future trading and diplomatic partners, yet relations with Washington were tricky: the Americans, engrossed in the miserable muddle of Vietnam, were resentful of Britain's reluctance to commit troops there in its support.

In 1968, Wilson was in his fifth year as prime minister. His reputation for knowing what was what, and for being rather better at economics than his predecessor, Sir Alec Douglas-Home, had suffered a severe blow with the 1967 devaluation. It had been ten years since the British were assured (by Harold Macmillan, in 1957) that they had never had it so good. Harold Wilson had been obliged to tell them, with all the frankness of a street trader, that their pounds were worth just as much as they ever had been.

Many people were still doing pretty well; the colour supplements were full of glossy advertisements, the boutique windows shimmering with multi-hued miniskirts and shirts, but the chilly winds of austerity were starting to give the country the shivers. Then, after De Gaulle's '*Non*' in March 1967 had come the November financial crisis. The pound's value against the dollar slashed from $2.80 to $2.40 – a 14.3 per cent devaluation. The country had to go begging for loans and credits, and in March 1968 George Brown stomped out of government, resigning as foreign secretary. Wilson may have been glad to see Brown go, choosing as his replacement the more amenable and much less volatile Michael Stewart. Yet neither Stewart nor Wilson could make any headway with the Rhodesian breakaway leader Ian Smith, nor could Wilson establish a warm relationship with US President Lyndon Johnson. Vietnam always stood in the way of their own special relationship – Wilson commenting that the Americans were desperate for any British support in Vietnam, even if it were only a pipe band. Wilson was keen to forge close ties with Washington, but was aware of left-wing rumblings in his own party, accusing him of being the presidential poodle. Then there were the student protests, the Kenyan Asian immigrants, and as the year unfolded, the Soviet invasion of Czechoslovakia.

Some aspects of 1969 seem familiar. Austerity chill gripped Whitehall and had spread across the country. Left-wing Labour MP Michael Foot (a future party leader) led an internal revolt against government spending cuts and wage controls, and the impact of a swingeing 1968 Budget: higher rates of investment surtax, corporation and purchase taxes, selective employment tax, increased duties on alcohol, tobacco, petrol and gambling, tighter credit controls. Inflation jumped from 2.2 per cent in 1967 to 4.7 per cent in 1968, though the bank rate did come down from 8 per cent in 1967 to 7 per cent by September 1968.

Unemployment had decreased slightly, to just over 500,000, but consumer demand was shaky. After the 1967 devaluation, Wilson had moved James Callaghan from the Treasury, bringing Roy Jenkins from the Home Office as his successor. In November 1968, Jenkins announced higher taxes and curbs on imports. Wage restraint, the government insisted, was essential for the country to weather the storm.

Through it all, Wilson remained outwardly imperturbable, still young, as prime ministers go, and apparently in good health. He was still only 60 when he quit, unexpectedly, in 1976, his later years darkened by illness. In 1968 though, his best years, he could tell himself, lay ahead. His rise to the top had been rapid: university undergraduate, Oxford don, wartime civil servant, then election as a Labour MP in 1945. By 1947 he was president of the Board of Trade, and the youngest Cabinet minister in the twentieth century to that date. In 1963 he succeeded Hugh Gaitskell as Labour Party leader, seeing off the challenge of his closest rival (and critic) George Brown. In 1964 he led Labour to power. With pipe and raincoat, Wilson's was hardly the image for the Swinging Sixties, but he embraced the changing times with gusto. It was all 'white heat of technology', Concorde, Post Office Tower, and being photographed with the Beatles, or with the England World Cup team in 1966. Britain was going to have more new towns, even a new city (Milton Keynes). The Transport Act (1968) injected new funding into public transport. There were to be new Passenger Transport Authorities, new bits of railway even; the first sections of London's latest Tube line, the Victoria Line (Walthamstow–Highbury & Islington, then on to Warren Street) were opened, though without ceremony – the Queen performed an official opening at Victoria the following year.

There might, Wilson dreamed, even be a new university open to all. The Open University (1969) would be regarded as one of his most successful achievements.

There was talk, too, of a third London airport … as much of an issue in the late 1960s as half a century later. The Roskill Commission was set up in

1968 to find a new airport site. It eventually narrowed the field to four new sites, one an offshore location in Essex, at Maplin Sands, near Foulness Island. Roskill eventually decided Maplin Sands was feasible, and more attractive in terms of environmental impact than sites in Buckinghamshire, Bedfordshire and Hertfordshire, though considerably more expensive. Nothing came of it: Maplin Sands was scuppered by the oil price crisis of the early 1970s, and instead London got a third airport at Stansted. This former Second World War bomber airfield had been growing charter flights during the 1960s and opened its first passenger terminal in 1969.

Wilson's personal popularity remained surprisingly high. He was more personable than the opposition leader, Edward Heath, more relaxed in the House of Commons, and a more accomplished TV performer. Wilson had mastered the art of the TV interview like no previous British prime minister. An appearance on BBC's *Panorama*, quizzed by Robin Day, held no terrors for him; he was calm, witty about opponents, fingertip loaded with facts and figures (when not massaging his pipe), and good-humouredly adroit at avoiding a direct answer whenever necessary. Many viewers, even those who voted against him, thought the prime minister reasonable, assured, competent. And who could doubt his intelligence? Yet they also rather liked his ordinariness: his support of Huddersfield Town Football Club, his fondness (according to wife Mary) for brown sauce, his Labrador dog Paddy, his family holidays in the Scilly Isles. The Queen was said to be quite taken with Wilson, who let her into his confidence more fully than some previous prime ministers, in audiences often lasting up to two hours.

So it was irritating, even for a student of philosophy (Wilson had read philosophy, politics and economics at Oxford) that events kept getting in the way. The 1968 Labour Party Conference proved tetchy, with unions unhappy about wages policy and rumours of pending industrial relations legislation – such as imposing compulsory strike ballots – as envisaged in the government's latest proposal, *In Place of Strife*. There were clouds over Northern Ireland, where the Stormont government was unpopular, and civil rights marches had led to clashes in Londonderry between Catholics and Protestants.

The military were unhappy about the withdrawal of British forces east of Suez. The Americans were grumpy. The French were apparently, in midsummer at any rate, about to have another revolution. At home, any economic good news (spending on housing, education, health, social security all up by over 6 per cent from 1963) was too easily swamped by gloom: productivity low (as ever), Britain's share of world trade falling, old standbys such as shipbuilding in what seemed like terminal decline from having been world leaders in 1950. No wonder the prime minister felt beset by troubles, and by enemies. His tendency towards paranoia was fed by whispers of a conspiracy in 1968, allegedly involving Cecil King, boss of the *Daily Mirror*, and high-profile figures from the establishment. King published an article in the *Mirror*, the country's biggest-selling daily paper (at 5 million copies), saying 'Enough is Enough'. It lambasted the prime minister as having lost all credit. The International Publishing Corporation reacted swiftly, and King was dismissed. The alleged 'coup' remains one of the mystery stories that swirl around Wilson's legacy.

Post-1968, the Wilson government stumbled on for two more years, before the prime minister went for an election in June 1970 – possibly hoping to catch Heath and the Tories on the hop, or perhaps because he was nervous about the public's reaction to decimalisation (scheduled for the start of 1971). He miscalculated; Labour lost, and rather to their surprise Edward Heath's Conservatives found themselves in office, but not for long. By 1974, Wilson, his pipe and his raincoat were back in Downing Street. 1968 had not been his finest hour, but the inscrutable smile had seen him through.

The mysterious death of the first spaceman

Yuri Gagarin has an assured place in the annals of spaceflight, the first astronaut into orbit, the first person to see the Earth from the alien void of space. That was in April 1961, and after a brief period of celebrity, when his smiling face was pictured all over the world, Gagarin had almost vanished from the public eye. Had he retired? Or maybe he was in training for an even more ambitious mission – a trip to the Moon, perhaps?

The announcement of Gagarin's death in March 1968 was almost anti-climactic, a sad and mysterious footnote to a career that had brought him a few minutes of breathtaking achievement, a year or so of fame, and then (perhaps, people could only speculate) years of frustration and relative obscurity.

The truth may never be known. The Soviet space programme in the 1950s and 1960s was shrouded in secrecy. Its origins lay in the bomb-blitzed German

Reich of 1945, when Allied scientists competed to grab what was left of Hitler's V-2 rockets. The Americans made off with the highest-profile German rocket scientist, Wernher von Braun, and other members of his team; the Russians took whomever they could, sending interrogators and experts to pick brains and retrieve rocket engine parts. Among the Soviet experts sent to examine unfinished V-2s and quiz captured German engineers was aeronautical scientist Sergei Korolyov, who had spent the war years under 'technical arrest', designing weapons for the Red Army. Now he was given the chance to test German rockets, far bigger than any experimental rockets flown before in Russia or America.

Korolyov's work on the V-2 led to improved developments of the German missile. It thus laid the foundations for the Soviet ballistic missile programme, as the Russians raced to catch up with the United States in the nuclear arms race, testing their own nuclear weapons and building large intercontinental ballistic missiles. Size mattered. The Soviet bomb was bigger and less sophisticated than the American, and so needed a much bigger rocket. This apparent technical inferiority handed the Russians a lead in rocketry that directly impacted on the space race, since Korolyov's team was able to modify big military missiles into heavy-lift launchers to send satellites and astronauts into space.

Yuri Gagarin was in his early twenties when in 1957 the world was rocked by news that Russia had launched the world's first Earth satellite. The 'beep-beep' radio signal from Sputnik 1 was an enormous shock to the Americans, whose space programme had been proceeding on the complacent assumption that the USA would get there first, even if the first US satellites would of necessity be tiny. The news that Sputnik 1 was the size of a football, and then that Sputnik 2 was big enough to carry a dog, caused a national outcry that sent the US space programme into overdrive to catch up. The Americans put up their first satellite in 1958, and announced a team of seven trainee Mercury astronauts in 1959. The race was on.

Then in 1961 the Russians again stole a march on the Americans, by putting the first man in space: a stocky, smiling fighter pilot named Yuri Gagarin. Gagarin was unknown before 12 April 1961. Born in 1934 in a town called Klushino (now renamed in his honour), he had flown fighter jets with the Soviet Air Force before, in 1960, joining the first selected group of prospective space pilots, known in Russia as 'cosmonauts'. Gagarin was reputedly a calm, methodical pilot: intelligent, and also short at 1.57m (5ft 2in) – again size mattered, given the cramped cabin in which he would fly into space.

No hints of the impending manned mission were picked up outside the USSR; a cloak of invisibility veiled the launch pad from prying eyes (and satellite surveillance in the 1960s was in its infancy, so not even the CIA had a clue what was about to happen). Soviet security paranoia had always kept everything about their space programme secret, unlike the Americans, who had cameras and TV crews to record every success (and failure). Gagarin's flight was over before most people heard about it; the news broke on Soviet radio, announcing the successful completion of the first ever manned spaceflight.

It had not been overambitious – just one orbit of the Earth, lasting 108 minutes – but it had been successful. Gagarin survived the launch, his body had coped with weightlessness, he had not become ill or gone crazy, and he had been the first human being to gaze down from space onto his home planet. He had spoken to ground control, but otherwise his activities while in orbit were necessarily limited (no eating or drinking, no TV link-ups, certainly no space-walking). He had reported no problems during the flight, telling ground control that all was going well and he was feeling fine.

If blast-off was a shatteringly perilous prelude to orbital flight, re-entry was an even more dangerous finale. Gagarin's sphere had seared a fiery path down through the atmosphere, stayed in one piece, and landed. So had Gagarin, though he baled out from the spacecraft at just over 22,000ft (7km) and floated down by parachute.

After this historic achievement came the publicity, and the apparently shy and modest Yuri Gagarin found himself a celebrity with nowhere to hide, the centre of world media attention. Now the Soviet authorities welcomed publicity, the better to celebrate this glorious triumph of socialist science. The world's first spaceman was paraded, garlanded, embraced by his Kremlin bosses, weighed down with medals, feted wherever he went. He was allowed to travel outside the USSR, in itself no mean reward, visiting Britain in July 1961 at the invitation of the Amalgamated Union of Foundry Workers (AUFW).

Whenever he was interviewed, he was asked when he was likely to go back into space. His reply was that he was eager to fly again, but he smiled at the speculative suggestions. A Soviet mission to the Moon, with Gagarin in command? A new super-spacecraft carrying several people? A Soviet space station in permanent orbit?

A polite smile. Nothing more.

Whatever the Soviet intentions, nothing came Gagarin's way for some time. While he fretted on the ground, other Russians journeyed into space, including the first woman, Valentina Tereshkova, in 1963, and in 1964 Gagarin's fellow cosmonaut Vladimir Komarov, who commanded the world's first three-man spacecraft, Voskhod 1.

Komarov was selected as mission pilot on the new Soviet spacecraft, Soyuz. Gagarin was also back front of stage, named as Komarov's backup. The Soyuz mission was scheduled for April 1967, and Gagarin would take the pilot's seat if Komarov got so much as a cold.

Komarov stayed sneeze-free, luckily for Gagarin, as it turned out. That first Soyuz flight ended in disaster. The orbit was, officially, trouble-free, although Western radio listeners picked up transmissions suggesting technical issues, including the later confirmed failure of a solar panel to deploy correctly. Whatever the cause, the craft had power and stability problems, leading ground control to end the mission early. In the circumstances, Komarov must have known as he prepared for re-entry that his chances of a successful landing were not good. He never made it. The official Soviet report on his death concluded that the capsule crashed to the ground after its landing parachute malfunctioned. Some Western experts speculated that Komarov may have been already dead before the fatal impact.

The Soyuz tragedy ended Gagarin's hope of further space flights. The Soviet space programme was halted while the Soyuz craft was redesigned, and during this period Gagarin lost his 'active' flight status. The reasons for this were never made clear, but it has been suggested the Soviet Government was fearful of risking the life of Russia's most famous son, should there be another accident. Gagarin was rumoured to be unhappy, even unstable. Or had he been affected by some mysterious space sickness?

In March 1968, the world learned that Gagarin would definitely make no more space flights: he had been killed in a plane crash while flying a two-seater MiG-15 jet. Gagarin and his fellow pilot Vladimir Seryogin had apparently been forced to take evasive action to avoid collision with a mystery object, probably a flock of birds or a balloon. The aircraft had gone into a tailspin and crashed. Both men were killed.

What was Gagarin doing flying around in a sedately unsupersonic trainer jet of late 1940s vintage? The official reason was that he was being refreshed as an air force pilot, after his years away on the cosmonaut programme. On the day of the accident, he had been scheduled to take up the MiG-15 three times: the first with the instructor, Seryogin, to be followed by two solos. The weather was poor, with wind and rain, and snow on the ground, and an account of Gagarin's morning claimed he had forgotten his ID, commenting on the bus taking fliers to the airfield that it was bad luck to lose your identity.

The fatal flight began just after 10 a.m. Gagarin was flying the MiG, and soon reported that he'd carried out the planned manoeuvres, including rolls and loops, and was coming home.

After that radio report, nothing.

Rescue teams found the wreckage of the jet on fire among trees. One body only was found, and identified as Seryogin's. Had Gagarin managed to eject before the jet hit the ground? Sadly not, for next day another body was found nearby, and identified as his.

Gagarin was given a hero's funeral and his body laid to rest in the Kremlin Wall, alongside heroes of the Red Revolution. Soviet supremo Leonid Brezhnev ordered a crackdown: no tittle-tattle, no rumour-mongering, nothing that might tarnish the reputation of the first man in space, or the competence of the Soviet Air Force. The investigators' crash report was to be top secret.

Naturally, conspiracy theorists soon got busy. There were allegations that Gagarin had become a heavy drinker. Or that he and his co-pilot Seryogin had flown the jet erratically, doing loops and other aerobatics for fun. Ufologists speculated on a close encounter with an alien craft, citing Gagarin's supposed belief in 'flying saucers'. The CIA got the blame in some quarters, as did Brezhnev himself. Some suggested that Gagarin might not have died at all, but had been spirited away, leaving an impostor corpse for the crash investigators.

None of these fanciful stories is likely to be true. What is sure is that Gagarin had found his meteoric fame hard to handle in the closed world of Soviet secrecy. For instance, it was ten years before the Soviet authorities confirmed that he had ejected from his spacecraft to land by parachute, a fact the cosmonaut is said to have confided to British test pilot Eric 'Winkle' Brown during Gagarin's visit to Britain in 1961. International celebrity had been a heady cocktail of tours, speeches, hotels, hospitality of all kinds. Gagarin's friends had noticed the change: the women, the drinking, the boyish grin less frequent.

After Komarov's death, Gagarin's chances of a second spaceflight were gone; for the Soviet leadership, he was too valuable a propaganda asset. Once he realised his cosmonaut days were over, Gagarin hoped to return to air force flying, which meant reverting to the more austere lifestyle of his younger days, retraining to rehone his sharpness as a fighter pilot, and then perhaps find solace in anonymity.

Two later theories provided alternative explanations about the 1968 crash. In 2010, Russian researchers blamed a failure in an air vent in the MiG's cockpit; sorting out this problem would have required the pilot to lose height quickly. The MiG went into too steep a dive, and the pilots blacked out, losing control of the plane, which smashed into the snow and trees. The plane had been fitted with external fuel tanks on the wings, and this additional load factor would have reduced its aerobatic capabilities.

Gagarin's fellow cosmonaut Aleksei Leonov, veteran of the first spacewalk, had another theory, involving a second, mystery aircraft. Leonov suggested that an ultra-secret supersonic Sukhoi Su-11, presumably on a test flight, had strayed into Gagarin's airspace. Its unexpected presence, probably at high speed, had forced the MiG to take evasive action, with catastrophic consequences. If so, an Su-11's presence was never made public.

Gagarin was 34 when he died. In 1969, the Apollo 11 astronauts left a medal in his honour on the surface of the Moon.

George bows out

On 15 March 1968, George Brown resigned as Britain's foreign secretary. It was the end of his career, not just as a government minister but as one of Labour's most recognisable political heavyweights. Few were surprised, since the Foreign Office was hardly a comfort zone for such an unpredictable figure, and Brown's time there had been turbulent.

George Brown had once seemed a likely Labour leader: energetic, bursting with enthusiasm and ideas, a stalwart of the party's right wing (pro-unions, anti-nuclear disarmament), born on a Peabody Trust estate in Lambeth and proud of it. A man of the people. An MP since the 1945 landslide, George Brown represented the Derbyshire constituency of Belper, and succeeded Aneurin Bevan as Labour's deputy leader in 1960. His early career in politics had been much influenced by Ernest Bevin, a trade unionist to his roots who had risen from humble origins to be foreign secretary. Brown's career had been almost the equal of his mentor's, and in the early 1960s he stood alongside Harold Wilson as the face of Labour. An adept campaigner, eloquent, excitable, though with a tendency to losing his temper and becoming over-exuberant, Brown had earned a reputation for fondness of a glass or three; it was perhaps his misfortune to lack a strong head for drink and not to realise the fact.

George Brown might have led the Labour Party. Following the sudden death of Hugh Gaitskell in 1963, Brown had come close to winning the leadership, but was defeated by the calculating and more temperate Harold Wilson – who also happened to be a former Oxford don, albeit from modest beginnings in Huddersfield. Brown's grudge against those with social or academic backgrounds different from his own was possibly confirmed by Wilson's success. But despite his disappointment at losing the leadership, Brown had campaigned energetically in Labour's 1964 election campaign, and was rewarded by Wilson with the post of first secretary in charge of the new Department of Economic Affairs.

Brown's grand vision of a National Plan for the British economy called for economic growth of over 3.5 per cent annually. He extolled the plan enthusiastically, in characteristically sweeping (and vague) terms. The general public had mixed views. Brown fans argued that the man 'spoke his mind', wasn't afraid to give an opinion, in contrast to so many politicians, including Wilson, who could cheerfully veil every unwelcome fact in a cloud of pipe smoke and ambivalence. Brown's plain-speaking style could also ruffle feathers; he could be loudly and obviously rude. An early US briefing note to President Kennedy had observed that this particular British politician was prone to irascibility and impulsiveness, as well as liking a drink.

In 1967, *The Times* had declared Brown 'a remarkable man', with at least some of the qualities that make a great statesman, though with reservations – Mr Brown was not perhaps the first person one would invite to take tea with a sedate and unworldly maiden aunt. Brown now felt even more the outsider.

Jim Callaghan was of similar background, but the two were not close allies, nor intimate friends. In Cabinet, Brown felt surrounded by too many Labourites he felt uncomfortable with and often disliked – Oxbridge-educated, middle-class 'intellectuals' who tended to regard some others in the Labour Party as illiterates.

In 1968, it all went wrong for George. He'd threatened resignation before, in 1966, when devaluation of the pound was first proposed then rejected by the Cabinet; Brown believed the economic austerity that Wilson preferred would seriously damage Britain's economy. Still grumbling, he had been reshuffled to the Foreign Office, and in 1967 devaluation had happened anyway. Becoming foreign secretary was an opportunity: Ernest Bevin had held the same high office, and with distinction, and as a convinced pro-European, Brown saw the chance to argue for a renewed British application to join the Common Market. A second approach was duly made, and once more rejected by De Gaulle.

Denied Europe, Brown cut an increasingly frustrated figure. The prime minister hogged the spotlight: it was Harold Wilson who went to Moscow in January 1968 for talks with Soviet premier Kosygin, Wilson who flew to Washington in February to see President Johnson. At the Foreign Office, the concerns seemed parochial – how to work out who did what, and who sat where, after the forthcoming merger with the Commonwealth Office; which notables to send to attend the independence celebrations in Mauritius and Swaziland; how to reassure Gibraltarians (again) that they would remain British; what to do about the intractable year-old civil war in Nigeria, where the federal forces under General Gowon seemed to be getting the better of the breakaway Biafran leader Ojukwu.

Brown's most successful initiative at the Foreign Office was as an author of United Nations Security Council Resolution 242, adopted in November 1967, and still seen as a key element in efforts to negotiate peace in the Middle East. The resolution called for Arab recognition of Israel's right to exist in exchange for Israeli withdrawal from occupied territories. Overall, though, his time at the Foreign Office was unhappy and marred by personal spats with officials – one row with the British ambassador to France ended in the ambassador's dismissal. Brown finally told Wilson that for personal reasons (hinting at marriage problems) he might have to resign, but when it came, his departure was after a final showdown with the prime minister over economic policy.

In March 1968, Wilson decided it might be a good idea to have an emergency bank holiday to relieve foreign pressure on the pound. So the prime minister called a meeting of the Privy Council. Brown missed the council; no one could find the foreign secretary, so the meeting went on without him. When he discovered this, Brown was furious, and there followed a stormy confrontation early in the morning. It was reported by Tony Benn (like Richard Crossman, a Cabinet diarist) that Brown 'shrieked and bellowed' at other ministers around the table, before tearing out in a temper, vowing never to serve under Wilson again.

There followed a letter to the prime minister suggesting it would be better if they part company. Wilson replied in his customary Janus-like manner, accepting Brown's 'resignation', but leaving the door at least partly open for Brown to change his mind – if Brown felt his letter had been misinterpreted.

Brown did not reply. The die was cast. He was out. And his career as a front-line politician was at an end.

Brown was soon out of the House of Commons as well. He spent most of the 1970 general election on the campaign trail, speaking for the Labour Party nationally, but scarcely bothering to seek votes in his own constituency. The result was that he lost the seat to a Conservative. Labour was defeated, and out of government, so Brown took a peerage, engaging in a long argument with the Garter King of Arms over the wording of his title as a lord. Wishing to retain his old commoner names, he finally settled for Baron George-Brown (of Jevington, Sussex).

The noble Lord George-Brown quit Labour for good in 1976, shortly before Harold Wilson (by then back in Downing Street) shocked everyone by suddenly resigning as prime minister, to be succeeded by Jim Callaghan. Press photos the day after Brown announced he was leaving the party showed him sprawled on the pavement ('out and down' ran one headline). Brown blamed new bifocals for the slip.

He later gave his support to the breakaway Social Democrats, after the SDP breach with Labour, but kept a lower profile. His long marriage ended in separation in 1982. When George Brown died in 1985, following a stroke, the obituaries were on the whole affectionate, a catalogue of 'might have beens'. Of course, George Brown admitted in an interview, there were times he wished he'd kept his mouth shut; times when, the morning after, he'd had second thoughts about the night before. He also said that while most British politicians had drunk too much or chased women too much, he had never been guilty of the second failing.

Massacre at My Lai

On 16 March 1968, US soldiers of a platoon from the 11th Infantry Brigade walked into a village in Vietnam. Theirs was one of a number of 23rd Infantry Division army units operating in Quang Ngai Province against the Vietcong guerrillas. The soldiers were in a grim frame of mind, for two days earlier some of their comrades had been hit by a booby-trap bomb, killing an NCO and wounding several other men.

Their next mission, the men had been told, was to enter the village of My Lai, an insignificant collection of homes amid the dense jungle, but believed to be a meeting place for local Vietcong. Entering the village, the American soldiers saw men and women cooking rice and preparing to go to work in their fields.

What happened next was the subject of, first, a cover-up, then revelation, inquiry, court martial and national heart-searching in the United States. My Lai turned into something worse than a firefight with a few guerrillas. Evidence later told of villagers being questioned, then shot. The massacre went on until around 11 a.m., by which time the village was in flames and most of its inhabitants dead. After the soldiers left, the Vietcong came in the night and buried the dead. Nearly two years later, US Army investigators uncovered mass graves containing several hundred villagers.

The official army report of the incident simply referred to it as yet one more encounter with the enemy with, fortunately, only one American casualty. Hugh Thompson, an army helicopter pilot, observed the shooting from above, and landed to try to halt it; he later filed a complaint about what he had seen of the ground troops' actions. The story of My Lai began to emerge only later that year when a discharged GI named Ronald Ridenhour, who had heard about the 'massacre' from other soldiers (though not there in person), started sending letters to President Nixon, to Congress, to the Pentagon, to anyone who would listen, demanding an inquiry. Investigative journalist Seymour Hersh made Ridenhour's allegations public in 1969.

General Westmoreland, US Army chief of staff, ordered an investigation; it did not report until March 1970, and recommended court martial charges against twenty-eight army officers. Only fourteen were charged and all save one were acquitted. The one guilty man was Platoon Commander Lieutenant William Calley Jr. It emerged that My Lai had been part of a US Army attempt to regain the initiative after the Tet Offensive, by organising a task force of infantry units to penetrate territory believed by the Vietcong to be 'safe'. 11th Brigade's commander had been keen for his men to get close to the enemy, not just to search, but to destroy. This included eradicating Vietcong support by burning villagers' homes, and by destroying crops, food supplies and wells. Most of the villagers, the troops were told, would have left for market by 8 a.m. The only people left in the villages, apart from the elderly and children, would therefore be Vietcong fighters or sympathisers.

About 100 US soldiers flew in and were landed by helicopters, before moving on foot into the villages. They apparently met no resistance. Then the killing began. Witnesses spoke of people being pushed into irrigation ditches before being shot; most of the victims were elderly, women or children.

Hardly any of this was made public during 1968, the year My Lai happened. The army did its best to cover up the massacre, even describing the incident as a victory, with few casualties. Information about the incident seeped out slowly, but as rumour and evidence coalesced into truth, the anti-war movement in the United States expressed outrage.

President Johnson had already decided he would not stand again; for the next president, Richard Nixon, the story would be one further piece of evidence to convince his administration that the war must be brought to an end. The incident, and the cover-up, revealed deep failings within the US Army's conduct of the war in Vietnam. People at home in the United States were shocked to be told of their troops' low morale, of a poor command structure, deep-rooted frustration and anger, and most were horrified by reports of widespread drug use by US troops. The My Lai Massacre was one more blot, for how could the killing of old men, mothers and babies be squared with a war supposedly being fought to defend freedom and democracy?

Lieutenant William Calley was the only soldier jailed. He received a life sentence in 1971, though this was later reduced to ten years, and he was paroled in 1974. Were there lessons to be learned? Most certainly. Were they learned? Future historians of the conflicts in Iraq, Afghanistan and perhaps elsewhere will judge.

4

April

DREAMS OR NIGHTMARES

The man died, not the dream

In American memory, 1963 and the killing of President Kennedy was still raw; the Vietnam War agony, which the late president had initiated by sending in US military advisers, had only intensified the national mood of doubt and soul-searching. The civil rights movement offered a beacon of hope; Congress was passing anti-discrimination legislation after President Johnson had got the 1964 Act through Congress following a seventy-five-day filibuster by opponents. That Act had compelled employers, unions, restaurants, hotels and other businesses serving the public to treat all people alike regardless of race, colour, religion or national origin. The 1968 Civil Rights Act had included the first legal restraints on discrimination in the sale and rent of housing.

And yet civil rights remained a burning issue, especially in the southern states of America, and the most prominent black civil rights leader, Martin Luther King Jr, had won wide support for his advocacy of non-violent action to secure those rights. His shooting in April 1968 was yet another moment of national tragedy.

President John F. Kennedy was shot in Dallas, Texas, on 22 November 1963. Only weeks before, an impressive civil rights march had taken place in Washington DC, and had been led by Dr King, founder six years earlier of the Southern Christian Leadership Conference, a non-violent movement against segregation, racism and discrimination. King had moved with his family to Montgomery, Alabama, to work as pastor at a church there, and had become a civil rights activist leader in 1955, the year of protests in Montgomery over the city's segregated bus system. The Montgomery bus boycott brought him national attention – the US Supreme Court ordered the city to end segregated seating for black and white passengers. Today, it seems an incredible issue to have to protest over, but this was the Deep South in the 1950s. As a consequence of the bus protests, King found himself, at the age of 26, in the national spotlight.

King continued to advocate peaceful protest, saying it was the only weapon his people had. The Kennedy presidency had achieved disappointingly little of substance in civil rights, until an outbreak of racial violence in Birmingham,

Alabama, was widely screened on television. Kennedy proposed a new civil rights bill. The 1963 March on Washington rally was organised in support of this legislation, and the occasion for the address for which King is most vividly remembered – his 'I Have a Dream' speech, delivered at the Lincoln Memorial in Washington.

Within two months of the speech, Kennedy was dead. Had King's dream died too? It seemed not, for President Johnson pushed on with the civil rights legislation enacted in 1964, and in recognition of his campaign, King received the 1964 Nobel Peace Prize. It was a moment for celebration and reflection. Yet the struggle was far from over. Deep divisions still fractured American society, most visibly in the city ghettos of Chicago or Los Angeles, and across the old racial battlegrounds of the Deep South. Impatience was reflected in certain more militant activist groups promoting 'Black Power' and adopting military-style language, while urging black men to reject the draft (conscription) and refuse to serve in the Vietnam War. In 1967 Muhammad Ali had refused to serve in the army, and had been stripped of his world heavyweight boxing title. He would not return to the ring until 1970.

In early April 1968, Martin Luther King Jr was in Memphis, Tennessee, having gone to support a strike by refuse collectors in the city. On 3 April he gave a speech, now remembered as 'I've been to the mountain top'. Next evening, he was staying in Room 306 on the second floor at the Lorraine Motel. While getting ready to attend dinner at the home of a local minister, King stepped out on the balcony of his room to speak to people gathered in the car park below. An unseen gunman was waiting.

At 6.05 p.m., Martin Luther King Jr fell, struck by a single shot to the head, apparently fired from across the street; he was rushed to hospital, but pronounced dead an hour later.

Civil rights leaders called for calm, but there were outbreaks of rioting as news of the tragedy spread across America. President Johnson declared 7 April a national day of mourning across the United States. On 8 April, Mrs Coretta King led a march through Memphis to commemorate her husband, and on 9 April Martin Luther King Jr's funeral was attended by political and civil rights leaders, including Vice President Hubert Humphrey. Over 100,000 mourners followed the civil rights leader through Atlanta, the coffin resting on a hearse drawn by a pair of mules.

The FBI led the murder hunt. Police found a rifle, hidden (not very well) next to a boarding house on South Main Street in Memphis, the apparent site from which the killer fired. Fingerprints found there matched those of a known fugitive, James Earl Ray, who had escaped from prison the previous year. Further evidence indicated Ray's presence in the boarding house and his occupation of a room that gave him a shooter's view of the Lorraine Motel. But there was no sign of Ray.

An international manhunt lasting two months tracked James Earl Ray to Britain, from where he was extradited back to the United States in July, and brought to trial. The accused pleaded guilty (though Ray later withdrew his confession) and he was sentenced to ninety-nine years in prison. Ray continued to insist that he had been framed. Subsequent investigations, including the Stokes Committee report of the US House of Representatives from 1976, suggested that Ray may have had accomplices and co-conspirators, but a 2000 Justice Department inquiry ruled there was insufficient evidence to support new investigation.

So who was the gunman?

Ray was a small-time crook, and in 1968 on the run, an escaped convict. He was cast as a lone gunman, like Lee Harvey Oswald, who shot President Kennedy in 1963, or Sirhan Sirhan, killer of Robert Kennedy later in 1968. Many did not credit Ray with the means, or the brains, for the assassination and suggested he was the fall guy in a conspiracy: the alleged conspirators being any of several groups to whom Martin Luther King Jr was anathema – white supremacists, the Ku Klux Klan, the Mafia, a whole distasteful menu of potential assassin sponsors. Conspiracy theorists also pointed the finger at the US establishment, including J. Edgar Hoover and the FBI, as well as the Memphis police.

At his trial, Ray at first pleaded guilty (to escape the death penalty), but three days later changed his story, claiming that he had been set up by a mystery man he knew only as Raoul. This shadowy figure had provided cash, a car, and instructions. Later there were stories and allegations of other gunmen and alternative 'killers': a man in the bushes, allegedly seen by one witness; a 'second gun', allegedly given to Memphis bar owner Lloyd Towers by an unknown man. The mysterious 'Raoul' was never identified, and was assumed by many to be a figment of James Earl Ray's imagination.

Ray's story was that he left Memphis soon after the King killing. He heard the news of the shooting on the radio, and learned police were looking for the driver of a white Mustang. Being in the vicinity of the motel, a prisoner on the run, and driving a Mustang, Ray decided to get as far away from Memphis as possible. He dumped the car, and took trains and buses to Canada. There he acquired a Canadian ID and a false passport, and on 7 May flew to London, and thence to Lisbon, with the intention of 'disappearing' in southern Africa, perhaps as a mercenary. However, on 17 May he was back in London, under the name 'Ramon Sneyd' and staying at a cheap hotel in Earls Court (rooms cost £2 a night). Money was a problem, for in June he apparently made two attempts at robbery in London: first at a Paddington jeweller's shop, whence he fled when the owners refused to comply with his demands, and then an unsuccessful hold-up at a branch of the Trustee Savings Bank in Earls Court.

Ray decided to try his luck in Brussels, to sign on as a mercenary, but on 8 June he was arrested at Heathrow Airport. An embarkation officer spotted that the man calling himself 'Sneyd' had two Canadian passports, both fake, and in different names (Sneyd and Sneya). Not surprisingly he smelled a rat. Ray was identified, arrested and extradited to the United States for trial.

Sentenced to ninety-nine years, James Earl Ray escaped from prison briefly, in 1977, but was recaptured after three days. He died in 1998, aged 70, in jail.

'Rivers of blood'

Few politicians are remembered by posterity for one headline-making speech alone. It is more remarkable for a politician to be remembered for a single phrase in a speech, albeit one as lurid as 'rivers of blood'. And even more remarkable of all when that precise arrangement of words did not appear in the speech at all.

Such was the fate of Wolverhampton MP Enoch Powell, for the speech he made in Birmingham in April 1968. As a classicist deeply versed in the literatures of ancient Rome and Greece, Powell would no doubt have found an appropriate Greek or Latin tag to epitomise his legacy. Where Martin Luther King Jr had spoken of a dream, Enoch Powell in this speech spoke of fear, uncertainty, even nightmare.

The 'rivers of blood' speech in 1968 ended Powell's career as a front-bench politician. It cost him a place in Edward Heath's Shadow Cabinet, and cast him in the role of rebel and right-wing icon/iconoclast – a role to which he was not entirely averse, but which he had up to 1968 tailored into an idiosyncratic communality with the Conservative Party and its leaders.

In a political career that had taken him to ministerial office, Powell had often been regarded by friends and foes alike with bafflement and amusement. His intellect made him a formidable opponent in debate, but most colleagues and commentators thought him too eccentric to be considered a future party leader (though this was certainly not Powell's own view of his prospects). He had never lacked self-belief. Born in Birmingham and educated at the city's King Edward's School, he had gone on to be a brilliant Cambridge scholar, and the Commonwealth's youngest professor (of Greek and in Sydney, Australia) before the war. In 1939 he had enlisted as a private, rising to the rank of brigadier (in Intelligence). His erudition was matched in youth by his ambition: while a student at Cambridge he expressed his hope of one day becoming Viceroy of India, a hope dashed when India became independent in 1947, and had no further need for viceroys.

Entering the Commons in 1950, as Conservative MP for Wolverhampton South-west, Powell had risen to junior ministerial jobs in Housing and the Treasury, resigned (with the Chancellor, Peter Thorneycroft, in 1958) but was restored to ministerial office as minister of health from 1960. He presented a somewhat anachronistic image even in the infancy of the new decade: dark-hatted, moustached, grimly austere but with a wolfish smile, he looked as if he'd walked in from a Cabinet of the 1930s. There was little of the Swinging Sixties about Powell, any more than there was in the style of the prime minister who promoted him, Harold Macmillan, whose frequent caricaturing as a grouse-shooting gent in Edwardian tweeds belied supreme political guile. In 1963 Powell had resigned again, this time in protest at the choice by the Conservative hierarchy of Alec Douglas-Home to succeed Harold Macmillan, when ill health compelled the prime minister to retire.

As health minister, Powell had been well aware of the influx of Caribbean workers, including nurses and doctors into the NHS, as part of the recruitment and immigration after the Second World War. The 1958 Notting Hill 'race riots' in London had been blamed on transitional adjustment problems – there were reports of discrimination and a 'colour bar' in rented accommodation and employment, concerns about 'mixed marriages', lurid press stories of crime, vice, drugs and slum landlords preying on immigrants. By the 1960s, well over 100,000 Afro-Caribbean people were living in London, with smaller immigrant communities in other cities such as Birmingham and Manchester. Even so, in much of the country a non-white face was still a novelty, and until 1968 most politicians had steered clear of immigration. However, the 1964 Smethwick election campaign had been shocking, with the Midlands constituency becoming a racist battleground, as Labour's Patrick Gordon Walker was beaten by the anti-immigration Conservative Peter Griffiths – though Labour later regained the seat in 1966. Before the 1964 general election, Powell had been asked what he thought was the most urgent issue facing the country. His reply surprised many. Immigration, he said. Not the economy, ailing infrastructure, defence, the colonial legacy, or Europe but … immigration.

Powell challenged for the Tory leadership after his party's defeat in the 1964 election, but came third, way behind Edward Heath. His reward was a place in the Shadow Cabinet as defence spokesman; in this role he took a clinical view of Britain's military role 'east of Suez' (unsustainable) and Britain's relationship with the United States (subordinate, yet blurred by an inability to come to terms with modern realities).

But in the spring of 1968 it was new legislation that occasioned his indignation, and changed his career. The date was Saturday 20 April, the week after Easter. Labour's new Race Relations Bill was due to have its second reading in the House of Commons on the following Tuesday.

The 1965 Race Relations Act had been a groundbreaker, setting up the Race Relations Board to deal with complaints of racial discrimination. The 1968 Bill, proposed by Home Secretary James Callaghan, was intended to extend the law. Its aim was to prevent individuals or organisations from refusing housing, employment or public services on the grounds of the applicant's ethnic background. It further proposed the setting up of a Community Relations Commission, to promote harmonious community relations and increase the power of the Race Relations Board. Callaghan told MPs that rarely had they faced an issue of greater social significance.

Immigration was back on the front pages, the result of an unexpected influx of Kenyan Asians. From the start of the year, numbers of migrants had been leaving Kenya and fleeing to Britain, citing discrimination by the Kenyan Government. They were of Asian origin but holders of British passports, and the Kenyan Government was now insisting that foreigners could hold work permits and operate businesses only until Kenyan citizens could be found to replace them. There had been demands that Asians running businesses in Nairobi and other cities in Kenya must hand over their enterprises to Africans, as part of the policy of 'Africanisation'. Charter planes had been filling up with Kenyan Asian families bound for London.

Alarmed at possible reaction to the arrival of large numbers of Kenyan Asians (albeit many of them successful business people), the Labour Government rushed through a new Commonwealth Immigrants Act in March. This restricted entry to the UK from Kenya to those who had a close connection with the United Kingdom, which in practice meant having relatives already resident. The Cabinet had split, some ministers opposing the new measure on the grounds that it was clearly discriminatory, but the government had pressed ahead with the Bill.

And then Enoch Powell spoke out. On 20 April 1968, he stood up to deliver a speech to the Conservative Association in Birmingham. Before the speech, Powell reportedly told a local journalist he thought it was going to make an impact. News filtered out. ATV got hold of an advance copy, and sent a television crew to Birmingham for the Saturday afternoon event.

Powell's speech started with some generalities; he declared the supreme function of statesmanship to be to provide against 'preventable evils', but that in seeking to do so, the statesman would meet obstacles deeply rooted in human nature.

So far, so general, and little to agitate the pencils of the local press.

But then things warmed up. Powell's speech included two anecdotal accounts of the supposed impact of recent immigration. A middle-aged working man had told the MP (Powell said) that given the chance he would leave the country, and urge his children to do the same. Powell saw this as indicative of 'the total transformation of a country', with by the year 2000 'approximately one-tenth' of its population being recent immigrants and their descendants. He declared this to be an issue about which 'I simply do not have the right to shrug my shoulders' and said it was madness to allow an annual inflow of some 50,000 dependants.

The new Race Relations Act, though not directly referred to, was clearly Powell's target. In his view, the government was conveying 'one-way privileges' in law upon 'the stranger, the disgruntled and the *agent provocateur*'. Someone claiming to be the victim of discrimination would henceforth enjoy legal rights denied to others. People (like the man he had quoted) were upset at being made to feel 'like strangers in their own country' as a result of decisions about which they had not been consulted. The legislation passing through Parliament, Powell said, risked 'throwing a match onto gunpowder', and he compared the situation with 'that tragic and intractable phenomenon which we watch with horror' – a reference to civil rights unrest in the United States, much in the news following the shooting of Martin Luther King Jr.

In a second anecdotal reference, the MP talked about a constituent: a widowed landlady in reduced circumstances who let rooms, but feared she now risked conviction for 'racialism'. Integration would not happen, he said, unless the law treated all the same (so if the regulations said all policemen must wear helmets, then all must wear helmets, whatever their background and cultural traditions). Giving groups 'special communal rights' would only fragment society further. The blame lay not with the migrants, who might be encouraged to re-emigrate if they chose, but with the government.

Slipping back into donnish mode, he made a fateful allusion to Classical literature, quoting the Roman poet Virgil's *Aeneid*. He did so in English (though he had considered quoting the original Latin), citing the prophecy of the Sibyl, who predicts 'wars, terrible wars, and the Tiber foaming with much blood ...'.

Powell said, 'As I look ahead, I am filled with foreboding. Like the Roman, I can foresee the River foaming with much blood.' And that was it. The 'rivers of blood' speech passed into history. Had Powell forgotten he was no longer in a Cambridge senior common room? Did he not realise the implications of such words, at a public meeting with the press in attendance? Or did he know exactly what he was saying? Whatever was the case, his words turned a run-of-the-mill party meeting into a national sensation.

The press seized not just on the 'blood' reference but on the whole tenor of the speech. *The Times* denounced it as evil; the *Sunday Times* called it 'racialist'. The very next day, Edward Heath sacked Powell from the Shadow Cabinet. While the media was largely hostile, and politicians chorused in disapproval, on the day after the speech a Gallup poll reported 70 per cent of respondents agreeing with Powell, and public demonstrations followed: 1,000 London dockers marched on Parliament Square, and were joined by Smithfield meat porters. Powell had suddenly become a rallying figurehead for anti-immigrant sentiment; his association with far-right views led even to comparisons with Oswald Mosley, the Fascist leader of the 1930s. While Powell was no demagogue, about to lead marches, many saw the 'rivers of blood' speech as imparting some kind of respectability and intellectual weight to racist arguments rightly confined to street corners. Opposition leader Edward Heath explained his decision to sack Powell on BBC Television's *Panorama*, declaring that the speech was inflammatory, and that the great majority of the British people did not share 'Mr Powell's way of putting his views in this speech'.

Mr Powell seemed unperturbed, almost bemused, by the furore, but he had become something of a pariah. He remained a Conservative MP, a prickly presence on the backbenches until 1974. That year there were two general elections, and in the first (February), Powell told voters to support Labour to defend British democracy. He was firmly anti-Common Market, and accused Prime Minister Edward Heath of being ready to sacrifice Britain's democracy in favour of membership of the European Community. The result was a hung parliament. Heath blamed Powell, and Powell quit the Conservative Party. In the second election of 1974 (in October) Labour won, but Powell was returned as Member of Parliament for South Down, as an Ulster Unionist, and he remained a Northern Ireland MP until 1987. He could never escape the impact of that 1968 speech, for he had become an unlikely icon for extremists, his image displayed on badges and T-shirts at anti-immigration meetings. After his death in 1998 the mere mention of his name continued to evoke responses from all sides.

Powell denied being a racist or 'racialist', but the damage was done. It was no good his arguing that he thought many Indians superior intellectually to Europeans. Former allies and political opponents alike concluded that his reputation was damaged because of his judgement, or lack of it: so often Powell had been the only person who seemed to know what he was talking about – a dangerous trait for any politician. The *Aeneid* quotation was (so his defenders claimed) included in the speech to communicate a sense of foreboding, nothing more. The headlines told their own story, and the speech remains one of the most hotly debated political events in 1960s Britain.

What's this, funny money?

Britain in 1968 was a cash-carrying society. There were more than 2 million cash registers and accounting machines, and roughly the same number of coin-operated machines, including phone boxes. People carried change for small transactions, like paying bus fares, and notes to spend in shops or garages. Money was so familiar that nobody thought twice about it. Yet within three years their loose change would look different and the pound be worth 100 new pence, not 240 old pennies.

Before 1968 everyone knew what cash looked like. Apart from minor changes, in banknotes particularly, Britain's currency had remained unchanged for generations. A Victorian penny might appear dark and smooth with wear, but it was recognisably the same as a new-minted penny, had the same value and with it a child could buy a penny chew in a sweet shop. So it was for the other coins in purse and pocket – the halfpenny or ha'penny, the threepenny bit, the tanner (sixpence), the half-crown and so on. You could trace history by the reigns of kings and queens. It was all there in the regal heads on coins.

But the times they were a-changin' at the Royal Mint. In fact there was a new mint, at Llantrisant in South Wales, opened in 1968 by the Queen. And it was about to mint new money. The government's decision to switch from pounds, shillings and pence to decimal currency had been made in 1966, but the first sign of the cash revolution came in 1968 with the appearance of the first decimal coins, the 5p and 10p, introduced to circulate alongside their 'doubles', the shilling and the florin (2-shilling piece).

Like most change in Britain, the monetary move had been subject to committee discussion and much havering. In 1961 the Conservative Government had set up a committee to consider the pros and cons of making the switch – the culmination of a debate that had started way back in the nineteenth century. It was agreed that decimalisation was rational, progressively modern, more 'European'. Britain's cash changeover was set for February 1971.

Advocates of change said it made sense. After all, most of the world used decimal currency already. Learning to add and take away in pounds, shillings and pence wasted time in school; having mastered maths in tens, children then had to learn to do money sums in a different way. Their parents and grandparents had managed well enough (and mastered obscure units such as gills and chains as well), but educational experts said everyone would be happier with a 10-based system, rather than struggling with a pound divided into 20 shillings each of 12 pennies. Shop staff would make fewer mistakes when giving change, and keeping accounts in two columns (rather than three) would save time and paper. Decimalisation would help trade, exports (even of cash registers) would benefit. Foreign visitors to Britain would no longer be baffled by the coins they were given.

But how to do it? The decimalisation committee had considered no fewer than twenty-five different systems before settling on two options – one based on 10 shillings, divided into 100 pence; the other on the pound, also divided into 100 pence. The advantage of the 10-shilling option, it was argued, was that one new penny would then have practically the same value as one old penny. But the 'ten bob solution' never stood a real chance, given the sentiment and familiarity attached to the pound, both domestically and internationally. The pound would stay. The new penny or 'p' would therefore be worth 2.4 old pennies. Shops would (it was hoped) adjust prices …

Some reformers wanted a new unit, the 'cent', to be the smallest coin, but the penny's long history (over 1,500 years) and popular sentiment counted in its favour. It too would stay. So in 1968 the first new 5 and 10 'new pence' coins began to turn up in change. Some welcomed them, gave them to children to keep. Others eyed and fingered the interlopers with a mixture of suspicion and distaste since the new designs were not universally admired. Cynics asked, was it all to do with this Common Market business? What about prices? What next? Beer by the litre, apples and pears by the kilo? Weighing up the shiny new 5p coins, some diehards concluded that this was almost as bad as having students rioting in the streets. Just like Paris …

5

May

ENGLAND SWINGS, PARIS ROCKS

The golden age of cool soccer?

Coolness was a quality to admire in 1968, though saying it was 'cool' usually meant it was time to pull on a sweater. Footballers like Best, Greaves and Young had a certain quality, however, in an era when the English and Scottish leagues abounded with star names. Jimmy Greaves, arch-poacher, scored goals for Tottenham with a precision that argued a razor-sharp brain as well as twinkling feet, while Everton's Alex Young played with an elegant artistry that led Greaves to describe him as 'Nureyev on grass'.

In 1968 'Nureyev' had danced across Goodison Park for the last time. After 275 games and 89 goals, Alex Young left Everton for Glentoran in Northern Ireland, eventually retiring with a knee injury to run a pub and later an upholstery business in Edinburgh. It was a classic end to a footballer's career for that day and age, even though the abolition of the maximum wage in 1961 had opened new horizons, with Johnny Haynes of Fulham becoming the first £100-a-week player in the English league. By 1968 George Best was earning roughly ten times as much, and had become the epitome of cool on the soccer pitch (and off it). His was the pop-star image of the game, an image enjoying a resurgence post-1966 and England's World Cup win.

The year 1966 had been a watershed for English football, with the World Cup triumph of Alf Ramsey's England team. Hopes had been high for further success in the 1968 European Championship (the new name for the European Nations Cup), but England went out in the semi-finals 0–1, after a bruising game against Yugoslavia, during which Alan Mullery was sent off for retaliation – the first England player to be sent off in an international. Manager Ramsey (by now Sir Alf) was so incensed by the Yugoslav tactics that he later paid Mullery's fine from the FA – £50. The 1968 champions were Italy, semi-final winners over the Soviet Union on the toss of a coin. In a prolonged final, the Italians and Yugoslavs failed to score after 120 minutes, so a replay was ordered, and this time Italy managed to find the net twice, winning 2–0.

Before 1967 no British soccer club had won the European Cup – the forerunner of today's Champions League. In 1967, Glasgow Celtic's 'Lisbon Lions' were the first British team to win Europe's foremost club competition. In

1968 Manchester United repeated the triumph, ten years after the Munich air crash that had destroyed the 'Busby Babes'. On 29 May, United took to the field at Wembley to contest the European Cup Final against Benfica of Portugal. There was a full house at the 'old' Wembley Stadium, where the souvenir programme cost just a shilling (5p). United's manager remained Matt Busby, a Munich survivor, and his 1968 team at Wembley included two other survivors of the 1958 tragedy: Bobby Charlton and Bill Foulkes. United's team that day was: Stepney (in goal), Brennan, Foulkes, Sadler, Dunne, Crerand, Charlton, Stiles, Best, Kidd and Aston. Scottish international Denis Law, injured, had to sit out the game.

The game itself was even with the scores level at 1–1 after ninety minutes, Charlton having scored for United, Graca for Benfica. So the match went into extra time, during which goals from Best, Charlton again, and Brian Kidd, 'babe' of the 1968 team at 19, won the game for United. It was an emotional day for the club and its supporters. Matt Busby afterwards wept, saying he felt winning had in some part justified the past, when travelling to play in Europe had cost the lives of so many of his 'Busby babes'.

Victory in the European Cup climaxed Busby's career. He was honoured with a knighthood, while the match showcased George Best to the world as one of the most inventive and mercurial talents in soccer. It was a golden year for the Northern Irishman, named European Footballer of the Year, and the British football writers' choice as their player of 1968. Just 22, George Best was Britain's first real soccer superstar, taken up by the media and as likely to be photographed leaving a King's Road club with a miniskirted model as on a muddy soccer pitch. His appetite for burning candles at all ends was sustained by huge natural talent and athleticism. His physique, wiry, even scrawny rather than imposingly muscular, held such grace and strength that he could shrug off bruising tackles to leave defenders trailing in his wake as he twisted and turned, dark mop of hair flowing.

The darker side of the story was yet to be fully revealed; 'booze, birds and cars' seemed to sum up much of it, but for a few years Best seemed to have it all, and be able to do it all. After he left Manchester United in 1974, he played for a number of other clubs, including the Los Angeles Aztecs and Fulham (alongside another showman, Rodney Marsh), and continued playing until he retired at the age of 37 in 1983. His later years were marred by personal problems, alcoholism, and ill health. He died in 2005.

1968 was a very good year for the city of Manchester, with United's rivals Manchester City winning the English First Division championship for only the second time in their history, pipping United by two points. Liverpool finished third and Leeds fourth. But Leeds also had a trophy, the Inter-City Fairs Cup, which they won by beating Ferencvaros of Hungary 1–0. They also won the League Cup, beating Arsenal by the same score. For Manchester City, co-managed by Joe Mercer and Malcolm Allison, the 1968 success brought the club's second-ever League title, with a team that included Neil Young, Colin Bell, Mike Summerbee and new signing (from Bolton) Francis Lee. West Bromwich Albion won the 1968 FA Cup, beating Everton by the only goal of the game, scored by centre forward and Hawthorns legend Jeff Astle. Astle was a classic, big centre forward of traditional type, with exceptional heading ability. Subsequently he has been cited as a victim of degenerative brain disease, his death at the age of 59 attributed to repeated trauma caused by heading the heavy leather footballs used in his day.

A survey of the 1968 leagues reveals the many outstanding players in action then. Both English and Scottish leagues were staffed almost entirely by British or Irish talent, with foreign imports (and players' agents) yet to come. A host of characters plied their trade on often muddy pitches at ageing and often almost dilapidated grounds; among them were Rodney Marsh, Frank McLintock, Terry Venables, Howard Kendall, Alan Ball, Ian St John, Tommy Smith, Colin Bell, Terry Paine, Jim Baxter, Dave MacKay, Derek Dougan … the list went on. Even suffering Fulham fans, watching their team relegated to Division Two in 1968, and then slide into Division Three the following season, had stars to watch, including former England captain Johnny Haynes and World Cup winner George Cohen. In two disastrous seasons Fulham went through four managers and forty different players – an unusually high turnover for the 1960s, when club loyalty and continuity meant more than it does in the modern Premiership.

The idea of attaching a sponsor's name to a soccer ground would have struck most football fans as odd – slightly more odd than having all-seat stadia. Old names were familiar signposts. Southampton played at the Dell, Sunderland at Roker Park, Stoke City at the Victoria Ground. The Baseball Ground said 'Derby', Boothferry Park 'Hull', Vetch Field 'Swansea' (still Swansea Town, not City as they became in 1969). On these and other grounds, from Gigg Lane

(Bury) to Vale Park (Port Vale), fans stood (or sat, if they were in the minority), stamped their feet to keep warm and pulled up their collars against the rain, pretty much as their fathers and grandfathers had done before them.

Paris in the spring

Paris might consider itself the city of artists and lovers, but in the spring of 1968 it was the city of rock-throwing, baton charges and revolting students. It was yet another French revolution. Or was it?

Trouble began on 2–3 May after the closure of the Nanterre campus of the University of Paris. This move by the authorities came after weeks of unrest and student agitation over education reforms, though some students were also demanding, less high-mindedly, that male and female students be allowed to sleep together in university accommodation.

Students and teachers at the old and prestigious Sorbonne met to demonstrate their solidarity with the Nanterre students, and demand an end to the police 'invasion' of university premises. The police were notoriously vigorous, especially the CRS (*Compagnies Républicaines de Sécurité* – the riot squad). Tensions began to rise.

On 6 May, the National Union of Students, with the university lecturers' union, jointly organised a protest march in the Latin Quarter of the city, bringing an estimated 20,000 people onto the streets. The police had by now taken control of the Sorbonne, and fought off the marchers' attempts to recapture it. The protesters set up barricades, hurled paving stones and were themselves assailed with tear gas and batons.

10 May was a day of upscaled violence, with cars used to block streets; the student leaders included 'Danny le Rouge' – the French–German activist Daniel Cohn-Bendit, who had been prominent in the original protest demanding free access to the women's dormitories. The students appealed to the trade unions for a general strike; the French Communist Party, led by Georges Marchais, was at first wary, regarding the students as bourgeois, spoiled children with anarchist leanings, who would soon enough forget their talk of revolution and scuttle back to manage their parents' businesses. The police brutality, though, brought about a hardening of resistance and protest across the Left. The unions became the students' allies, seeing an opportunity to pile

further pressure on the Gaullist prime minister Georges Pompidou, who had been in the post since 1962 – an eternity in French politics.

While the would-be revolutionaries declared the Sorbonne a commune, unrest spread to other universities. On 13 May, the day of the general strike, it was estimated that 800,000 people were on the march through Paris. Doctors, lawyers, shop workers and civil servants had joined the protest. Marching crowds called De Gaulle 'an assassin' and compared the hated riot police, the CRS, with the Nazi SS. Was this really a revolution, like the one the Beatles were to sing about? For a brief while the turmoil seemed to be Europe-wide, with enigmatic graffiti appearing, such as 'the future is what we put into it now'. Intellectuals analysed the protests to judge if there really was a global freedom movement, looking at what was happening, or about to happen, in Czechoslovakia, and at the civil rights marches in the United States. Even in West Germany, student activists were calling for the Bonn Government to 're-engage' with the Communist East, and demanding that 'Nazis' be hounded out of universities and government posts.

There were demonstrations against the Communist regime in Poland (January to March), centred on the University of Warsaw. As a result the government shut down all Polish universities and accused protesters of being 'Zionists'. In Sweden, protesters demonstrated against South Africa's participation in sport, as did students in Mexico ahead of the Olympic Games. Spanish students called on General Franco to restore democracy, and so Madrid University was closed for a month; a protest in Rome led to a similar closure of education facilities there. There was even a small demonstration in Moscow, in August, by a group who staged a protest against the Soviet invasion of Czechoslovakia; their treatment was predictably unsympathetic: beatings, arrest and jail.

Britain's youth remained comparatively calm: there were anti-Vietnam War protests, the most eye-catching when crowds filled Grosvenor Square in London to besiege the US Embassy, and the media showed interest in the Euro-revolutionaries, particularly Cohn-Bendit. Lacking from the British protest scene was the blending of student energy and indignation with trade union agitation. Protesters were energised by a range of causes, including the environment, sexual freedom, racial discrimination and feminist issues. In September 1968 a protest by American 'women's liberation' activists against the Miss America beauty pageant received substantial media coverage.

The situation in France continued to deteriorate as May wore on. On 24 May students got into the Paris Stock Exchange, raising the red flag and attempting to set the building on fire. That night, a policeman was killed – the first fatality. On 29 May, President De Gaulle travelled for a secret meeting at Baden Baden with General Massu, who commanded French military units in West Germany. De Gaulle did not bother telling his prime minister, but received assurances from the general of the army's support, should it be needed to quell any further insurrection.

As it turned out, the army was not required. The students were being nudged to one side by the professional agitators, chiefly the trade unions, led by the CGT (*Confédération générale du travail*), and politicians of the Left. Prime Minister Georges Pompidou had met union bosses (25–27 May) and they had drawn up the Grenelle Agreement, which gave concessions to the unions (and a rise in the minimum wage). Pompidou found some union bosses fearful that they too might be swept away by student extremists, now described as anarchists and Trotskyites. And De Gaulle was cheered by evidence of a counter-revolution, as Gaullist supporters now took to the streets to complain about the disruption.

It was not to be the Paris Commune of 1871 all over again. France in 1968 was more robust, and self-confident, not in the throes of self-analysis after a crushing defeat by an old foe (Prussia in 1870, Germany in 1940). Even if most students regarded their president as so far out of touch with modern life as to be a museum relic, De Gaulle could still draw on a deep well of support out in the country. He had abandoned his initial gloomy thoughts of retirement, and on 30 May broadcast a stern appeal for a return to law and order. The temperature was dropping. The unions pulled back, uneasy at what might have been let out of the bottle, and the middle classes made their voices heard more loudly.

After two weeks, the strikes came to an end. Intermittent student protests continued until mid-June, but agitation was banned on 12 June, and on 14 June the remaining students occupying the Sorbonne were evicted. De Gaulle suggested a referendum on the proposed Grenelle concessions. Pompidou argued for fresh general elections instead, to secure the government's position, and he was right. The June 1968 election gave the Gaullists a thumping majority, reinforcing their hold on the National Assembly. Pompidou had his own future agenda, and resigned on 10 July.

While the unions got their wages and conditions deal, the students had to be satisfied with educational reforms. De Gaulle, though, had had enough. His eleven years at the Elysée Palace were almost over, and the French public on the whole were not sorry to see him go. The 78-year-old general now seemed an obstacle to progress, rather than the saviour of the republic. After losing a referendum on constitutional reform, De Gaulle resigned in April 1969, and within three months Georges Pompidou had seen his plan succeed, as he became France's new president. By the end of the following year, De Gaulle was dead.

'England Swings (Like A Pendulum Do)'

So sang American Roger Miller. Americans, and others, were entranced and confused by the apparent transformation of Britain by what people had begun to call 'youth culture'. The late 1940s and early 1950s in London were described by Roy Porter as London's 'Indian summer', the city slowly shaking off the dust and grime of six years of Blitz and attrition, shortages and neglect. There were still big ships moving in and out of the London Docks. There were trams and trolleybuses and smoking chimneys causing impenetrable and life-harming 'pea-soup' smogs. Small side streets could still be playgrounds for city kids; they had not yet become car rat-runs or all-day car parks, with houses attached.

By 1968, the 1950s had been consigned to history, but not yet to nostalgia. The older generation could see things were changing, not what they used to be, but that was progress: supermarkets, burger bars, bowling alleys, colour television, parking meters, miniskirts and long hair. A shame to say goodbye to trams and steam trains, but then so many families could run a car nowadays – the number of cars had more than doubled between 1958 and 1968.

London was swinging – the newspapers said so. The rest of the country was doing its best to catch up, and swing too, without everyone being absolutely sure how. Not everyone approved of all the changes. Things were more 'permissive', a new word that covered various behaviours, from divorce and homosexuality to women smoking in public and wearing dresses that, by 1968, ended high above the knee. 'Middle England' was still digesting the sexual revolution, highlighted by the legalising of abortion and homosexual acts (between consenting adults) by Labour in 1967.

London was exporting people: the population of Greater London shrank by 7 per cent. There were in fact two Londons. One was the swinging city of 1960s mythology, symbolised in a way by the appearance in 1968 of a new magazine, *Time Out*, which had declared its intention of telling readers 'where it's at'. Teen magazines (*Rave, Honey, Fabulous 208, Jackie*) and the music press (*Melody Maker, New Musical Express*) presented an image of a young country infatuated and exhilarated by pop stars, footballers, interior design, longer hair and shorter skirts. The colour supplements of the heavyweight newspapers, such as the *Sunday Times* and *The Observer* added extra punch, showing all that was brilliant, and shiny, and breakthrough-new in the old country.

By the late 1960s, youth (or most of it) had been enfranchised economically, with jobs plentiful, unemployment low, and real earnings still on the rise, as they had been in the two decades since the war. The young were also free from National Service (conscription), which had ended in 1960, and many more young men, and women, were going to university, the older redbricks and the new institutions opened in the 1960s. Students with grants (not loans) were not exactly well off – a typical grant amounted to little more than £100 per term – but tuition was free, and it was surprising how much fun could be had on a fiver a week.

Five pounds would not go very far, however, along the King's Road, where high-end fashion was leading the way towards very conspicuous consumption. It was here that Mary Quant had run her shop Bazaar since 1955, and then burst upon the scene in the mid-1960s with the miniskirt. The King's Road remained the Mecca for the fashionistas, especially young women with money or those of either sex who wished to brush shoulders with the moneyed. Carnaby Street, on the fringe of the still disreputable Soho, was altogether more commercial and, after a brief flurry of authentic cutting-edge Mod retailing, it became mainly a street market for tourist tat. London's art schools and colleges produced fashion designers keen to emulate Mary Quant, and artists and designers to create dazzling album sleeves and posters, or fashionable household goods to be sold to the upwardly mobile by stores such as Terence Conran's Habitat, which opened its first Fulham Road store in 1964.

Suits and ties were still in, but less cool by 1968 than at the start of the decade, when the Mods had opted for the trim and neat suited look (albeit underneath a parka if riding a scooter). The suit/leather clash between Mods and Rockers of the early 1960s had been washed over by a hazy, flowery floppiness. Hairstyles were longer, girls' hemlines shorter, and 1967's 'summer of love' in the United States had inspired celebrations of peace and love in a mood of hazy but gentle silliness. At the same time though student protests and the anti-Vietnam War movement were sending others out onto the streets. The rock and peace festival that made New York's Woodstock famous was still in the planning stage for the following year, but Britain had its own fledgling rock festivals, even if summer days and nights were seldom warm enough for kaftans and bare torsos. The Beatles were also doing their bit, by starting their own record label, and making the right noises for world peace by jetting off to India to visit the Maharishi, with their entourage, to meditate. Getting in touch with one's inner self was almost obligatory if you wanted to stay with it, since the world (and especially the media in the United States) regarded England/London/Liverpool as an amorphous vortex of creativity: psychedelic, super-cool and 'swinging'.

Ronan Point

The swinging aura of London marked a steady change in its economic heart. The city was steadily losing its manufacturing activity with the closure (by 1970) of the AEL and Park Royal bus works, and the steady decline of the once busy industrial belt. Employers such as Fairey/Westland (Hayes), GEC (Willesden) and Lucas (Acton) reduced their inner London workforces and some factories either closed or moved further out – many moving east towards Romford or west towards Reading and Basingstoke. Even some of the big city insurance companies, such as Sun Alliance, were on the move, as too were government departments in a bid to cut costs, stimulate regional development, and relieve inner city overcrowding.

The docks – for so long London's very visible and emotive trade link to the world – were going. As recently as the 1950s, up to 1,000 ships arrived each week in London's docks, but by the mid-1960s London was no longer the pre-eminent port of Empire, and no longer so well placed to profit from shifting trade preferences and geographic and political orientations. The East End docks had not been modernised adequately after the war. With their obsolete and restrictive working practices, they (and other docks such as Liverpool) faced stiff competition from modern European container ports such as Rotterdam, and new ports giving onto the North Sea, such as Lowestoft. Dock strikes and militancy among union leaders had not helped, and in 1967 the closure process had started with the East India Docks. One by one the docks, which in the 1950s employed 30,000 people, closed down, along with associated businesses. 1968 saw a lull in dock closures, but in 1969 St Katherine's Dock was also closed, and by the 1980s all the docks had gone. It was hard to foresee back in 1968 the transformation of 'Docklands' into the city's second financial trading hub, or the parallel changes to the East End landscape and communities that once surrounded the docks, and London's river.

Post-war home building was ring-fenced in London's case by the Green Belt. New towns such as Stevenage and Harlow were growing fast, and every borough within the Greater London Council area had its plan for more housing. The profiteering private landlord had become a public enemy, following one particularly notorious case involving a property owner named Peter Rachman (who died in 1962, but was later named as being involved in the so-called Profumo Affair). Legislation to regulate tenancy arrangements had brought about a shift in the market, ending the era of widespread 'rooms to rent' and taking in a lodger.

More people wanted their own homes, and as demand for accommodation grew, some councils happily took on the role of main housing provider. Streets of Victorian terraced homes were bulldozed, councils arguing that it was more economical to replan and build anew than to refurbish, for example, by putting in the bathrooms and inside toilets like most residents wanted. Architects' paper dreams captivated local authority planners, so up went high-rise blocks as the 'slum-clearance' programmes proceeded. Demolition destroyed old communities while the new tower block estates rose across London and other cities from the early 1960s. They were to prove no utopias.

Streets in the sky seemed fine on paper. But what if the lifts went wrong? Or the rubbish chutes became blocked, and rat infested? Where would people meet, chat, hang out their washing, watch the children playing? The problems of high-rise life were accentuated in 1968 by the collapse of Ronan Point, on 16 May 1968.

Ronan Point was a tower block in Newham, twenty-two storeys high. The building had been started in 1966, completed in March 1968 and its residents had lived there for just four months. An explosion on the eighteenth floor, from a kitchen gas leak, led to the entire block collapsing, as if a child's breath had scattered a house of cards. The building design, employing a factory-built system, was so inadequate that a modest gale force wind of 60mph (97km/h) would have had a similar disastrous effect. This was the finding of a later public inquiry.

The inquiry, in August 1968, found that the gas explosion had triggered the collapse of the 'system-built' structure. Its design was unsound. The block was assembled by bolting together prefabricated concrete panels. Joints had been stuffed with newspapers, not concrete, and each wall panel was resting on bolts, rather than on beds of mortar, with rainwater able to seep into joints. The bolts took the strain for the whole building, resulting in pressure-cracking of concrete wall panels.

The inquiry concluded that the disaster was caused when, in her flat on the corner of the eighteenth floor, Mrs Ivy Hodge lit the gas to make a cup of tea. She was lucky not to have been killed when blown across the kitchen. The explosion took out the outer walls supporting the four flats above; as these walls fell away, the floor above collapsed. Three of the four flats above the explosion site were empty. Four people died and seventeen suffered injury. Families fleeing their homes had to negotiate the stairs, since the lifts had stopped working.

Ronan Point has been called modernist architecture's *Titanic*. Following the inquiry, British standard structural design codes were introduced, and regulations tightened, with the aim of ensuring that no similar new-built structure would suffer collapse as a result of wind, explosion or vehicle impact. The new regulations were applied to all buildings over five storeys constructed after November 1968, to ensure they were able to resist an explosive force. The gas supply was removed from the rebuilt Ronan Point and other blocks on the estate; blocks of similar design were switched to all-electric cooking and heating. Ronan Point, rebuilt, lasted until 1986 when it was demolished to be replaced with low-rise terraced houses.

The Ronan Point disaster might have ended council planners' love affair with high-rise, encouraging a shift to 'low-rise, high-density' residential schemes, and even some attempt to reproduce traditional city patterns (or lack of pattern). Public enthusiasm for high-rise living was significantly diminished. The scandal was one more negative for tower-block estates too often associated with stories of vandalism, resident isolation and poor maintenance – stories that tarnished the gloss of architects' imaginings. Victorian and Georgian homes that had escaped demolition were now more likely to be 'improved', and in many London locations have become such desirable properties that their sale prices today would be unbelievable to former 1960s residents. But Ronan Point did not mark the end of tower living, nor of tragedies linked to building design and materials, as the 2017 Grenfell Tower fire disaster in North Kensington made all too tragically clear.

Crime and retribution

Peace and love may have been in the air, along with the music of meditation, but not everyone was wholly focused on their inner being. Old-fashioned criminality had not gone away. Protesters might complain about the law, the judges, the police – so apparently out of sympathy with the changing times, so out of touch with the 1960s world of love-ins, sit-ins, sleep-ins or anti-war lie-downs. Yet just around the corner, as always, were the serious criminals. Away from the discos and demos, the dancing and chanting, was another, darker, world. And dimly perceptible through the hazy conviction that the young had found the key and cracked the code to reveal the existential truths about love, sex, inner peace and spiritual oneness with the universe was an unpleasant old reality: the fat slug beneath the stone – organised crime.

The underworld in the 1960s did much as it had done for most of the twentieth century: made money in the same old ways (prostitution, drugs, gambling, extortion, protection, robbery with or without violence, fraud, forgery …). The big city gangs controlled crime on their 'manors' and bargained or occasionally jostled with rivals over lucrative turf, dishing our retribution and punishment, often violently, whenever they felt a boundary had been crossed.

The police, especially the Met in London, knew their local villains pretty well, despite the shift from bobbies pounding the beat to coppers in cars, as shown on television. They were perhaps more comfortable with old-style villains than with more modish law breakers such as drug-taking pop stars and student protesters, and they had an uneasy relationship with London's ethnic minority population. Trendy liberals thought it ridiculous that police should waste their time arresting pop stars for smoking pot. Why didn't they concentrate on catching criminals?

In 1968, the police had two moments for self-congratulation, and a good press, with approving headlines for once. The good news was twofold: the arrest of two of London's most notorious gangsters and the capture of the man regarded as the leader of the Great Train Robbers.

The gangsters were the Kray twins, Reggie and Ronnie. With their older brother Charlie, the Krays had built up the most feared gang in London's East End, in the process turning themselves into dinner-jacketed celebrities mingling with actors, singers and the odd louche politician in West End clubs. The twins' brushes with the law had begun in 1952, when as teenagers they had been conscripted for National Service. Quickly finding army life not to their taste, they kicked off a rumpus (both were boxers) and walked out to go back home. The army arrested them, but gave the twins a rapid dishonourable discharge, glad to be rid of them. Graduating into serious crime, the Krays by the mid-1960s were the uncrowned kings of London's underworld north of the Thames, seen in the West End rubbing shoulders with the establishment. Few dared to cross the Krays, or their allies, and the press kept its distance from the real truth of their activities.

The police knew a good deal about the Krays, particularly regarding the rivalry between the Krays, north of the Thames, and the Richardson gang, in south London. Knowing was one thing; catching and getting witnesses to testify in court was quite another matter. Two particularly brutal gangland killings had made news in recent months, and put the police under more pressure to make arrests: first the shooting in 1966 of George Cornell, then in 1967 the stabbing to death of Frank 'The Hat' McVitie. The CID suspected the Krays, but could they prove it? There was also the mystery of missing Frank Mitchell, the so-called 'Mad Axeman'. A 'lifer' in Dartmoor since 1962, the ultra-violent and unpredictable Mitchell had been helped to escape in 1966 – by persons unknown. His instability must have made him a troublesome house guest. No one knew where he was. The best guess was he had been 'eliminated'. The Krays were prime suspects. But could the police hold them for it?

In May 1968, detectives leading the pursuit of evidence against the Krays finally got their men. Detective Inspector Leonard 'Nipper' Read was able to arrest the twins and members of their gang, and bring them to court. At their trial (in 1969), Reggie and Ronnie Kray were found guilty of the McVitie killing; Ronnie and another man were convicted for the Cornell murder.

Separately, the twins were cleared of murder in the case of Frank Mitchell, for lack of evidence. Subsequently it was claimed that Mitchell had indeed been killed and his body thrown into the Channel. Reggie Kray was, however, convicted of enabling Mitchell's escape from Dartmoor. The judge handed down sentences on the twins of thirty years; their brother Charlie Kray received a ten-year sentence.

And so the Krays left the London clubs and gangland scene, though not public consciousness, as their story was told and retold in books and on film. Ronnie Kray died in Broadmoor Prison Hospital in 1995 at the age of 61. Reggie Kray was finally released from jail in August 2000, by then terminally ill with cancer, and died just weeks later. Brother Charlie left prison in 1975, but was later jailed again for other offences, and died in prison in 2000.

The arrest of the Krays was an event to celebrate at Scotland Yard, although satisfaction was tempered by anxiety about the trial's outcome. Awaiting it, detectives could raise a glass to another success in January: the recapture of Great Train Robber Charlie Wilson. In November 1968 they had more good news – the arrest of the alleged leader and co-author of the 1963 mail train robbery, Bruce Reynolds.

The 1963 Great Train Robbery had been the crime sensation of that year, and much dwelt on ever since. A team of crooks had planned and executed the interception of the London to Glasgow mail train. In August, at dead of night in rural Buckinghamshire, the robbers had halted the train to make off with £2.6 million (well over £40 million in modern cash terms). The nature and style of the heist had invested the Great Train Robbers with a cavalier glamour that was undeserved; nor were they Robin Hood outlaws. The fifteen or so gang members (the exact number was never clear) were in it for the money, of which the principals' share was about £150,000 each. Newspapers treated readers to detailed accounts of the gang's plan, which involved using a fake red light to stop the train, and recruiting a driver to move it. This had gone awry when the driver found he could not operate the locomotive type, so the money had to be manhandled to the gang's getaway lorry. Less attention was given to the mail train's driver, Jack Mills, who was hit on the head and seriously injured during the robbery.

After the theft, the Train Robbers had fled, but not far or fast enough. Most were swiftly traced and arrested. At the beginning of 1968, only three high-profile Train Robbers were still at large: Ronnie Biggs (a minor participant, out of reach in South America), Charlie Wilson, and leader Bruce Reynolds, known to the gang as 'Napoleon'.

Wilson had been the gang's 'treasurer', responsible for sharing out the loot. A long-time criminal associate of Reynolds, he had been caught only nine days after the robbery in August 1963, following a tip-off leading police to the gang's hideout at Leatherslade Farm. He refused to talk when questioned and was sentenced to thirty years. In 1964, Wilson had broken out of Birmingham's Winson Green Prison, and been on the run ever since. His life as a fugitive had taken him to Canada, to reunions with Reynolds, and also to France. In January 1968, the police caught up with Wilson in Canada; he was brought back to England and returned to jail, in the high-security wing at Parkhurst on the Isle of Wight.

Reynolds had got clean away in 1963. Using false names, he had lived in France, Canada and Mexico. By 1968 he was running low on funds and risked returning to Britain, renting a house in Torquay under the name of Keith Miller and presumably hoping that now the dust had settled he could pick up where he had left off and re-establish links with old contacts. One of those contacts may have talked, because the police came calling and Reynolds was arrested at his Devon Riviera villa. He, too, got thirty years.

The 1968 arrests of Wilson and Reynolds were almost the last fanfare in the police hunt for the Great Train Robbers. Ronnie Biggs remained a tantalising fugitive, visible in Brazil but out of reach for thirty-six years. Eventually he returned to Britain, where he died in 2013, nine months after attending the funeral of Bruce Reynolds. By that time Charlie Wilson was long gone – murdered in 1990 by a hitman on a bicycle in Spain.

6

June

YOU WANT A REVOLUTION?

Sit in to get out

Youth culture took firm hold in the 1960s. It even received official recognition with, in November 1968, its own government minister. Judith Hart, one of senior government's few women portfolio holders, was officially Paymaster General, and previously minister for social security. Her new brief was wide-ranging: it covered all youth problems, including those of Britain's students. Some of those students – home-grown and from abroad – had caused a few headaches earlier in the year.

British students at that time included those studying at training colleges and other further education institutions. The number was less than 400,000 – under 6 per cent of the population. Most of these seemed more anxious to have a good time than go on protest marches, but Vietnam was a flashpoint, just as the Cuban Missile Crisis of 1962 had been and before that the CND (Campaign for Nuclear Disarmament) 'Ban the Bomb' marches of the 1950s. Britain had stayed out of the Vietnam War and Harold Wilson had urged President Johnson to find a way to peace talks, but British influence was minimal. The main concern of the British Government was to prevent anti-war protests at home becoming disruptive and a focus for student revolt. Quite what 'student power' meant exercised older minds. Were the youthful protesters tools of international Marxism? Or Soviet chicanery? Were they anarchists or Castroists? Or simply young people led astray by pop songs, cannabis and casual sex?

On 17 March 1968 trouble flared in London's Grosvenor Square, an elegant Mayfair location dominated by the US Embassy, and the eagle that adorned its front (a building sometimes described as reminiscent of 1930s Berlin). The anti-war protest held that day in the square led to violence, with 200 demonstrators arrested, and almost 100 injured, many of them police. Unrest was simmering in France, too, before the summer explosion of 'student power' in Paris, but Britain's universities seemed on the whole less revolutionary than their continental counterparts, or those in the United States. Education minister Edward Short blamed Americans for inciting student agitation, encouraging pot smoking, free love and other undesirable activities. It was essential to be on the alert for any whiff of 'student power' ideas infiltrating

British universities, and to monitor visiting radicals, some of whom were arriving to tour British universities.

British students were, on the whole, still respectably attentive to beer drinking, parties, debates and even pursuing their studies. Most 'ordinary' people regarded students as a privileged minority, clever boys and girls, many from grammar schools, and probably the first of their families to go to university (not yet 'uni'). Protests by French students at the Sorbonne inspired a copycat sit-in on 23 May at the London School of Economics, and on 28 May students occupied Hornsey College of Art in north London. But this was as nothing compared to what was going on in Paris, where televised reports showed students in violent confrontation with the police. The government waited anxiously for further signs of British infection with the Continental anarchy virus, but apart from these modest disruptions, all seemed remarkably docile. At Bristol some students opted to set up a 'free university', inviting anyone to join who had a shilling (5p). There had also been a minor brouhaha at Cambridge, when a student tried to interrupt a Senate function, and had to be removed.

Otherwise, all calm – but before the storm?

Onto the scene walked a German student radical, known in the press as Danny the Red or 'Danny Le Rouge'. (In Britain this meant he was at times confused in print with the drag entertainer Danny La Rue.) Daniel Cohn-Bendit (23) had been invited to London to take part in a BBC documentary focusing on international student unrest. He had been a leader of the initial protests at Nanterre, about 'living conditions' – a key issue being the rule barring men from visiting women students for the night.

By now, Danny the Red was a media celebrity, a Maoist anarchist who helpfully spoke fluent English as he denied he was planning world revolution. He arrived in London on 11 June, expressing a wish to visit Highgate Cemetery and Karl Marx's grave there, but with his trademark red hair apparently dyed black. Casually he mentioned perhaps seeking political asylum. Tariq Ali, former president of the Oxford Union and co-editor of the left-leaning 'underground' publication *Black Dwarf*, was there to greet Cohn-Bendit at the airport, whence he was driven in a BBC car to a party at which the guests included theatre critic Kenneth Tynan.

Cohn-Bendit then asked for his permit to stay to be extended – or he would not make his scheduled BBC appearance. Other international students gathered around to sing the Communist anthem, the Internationale, in the BBC foyer. Cohn-Bendit then went off to Highgate Cemetery, there to sing the Internationale again to the spirit of Karl Marx. The Home Office duly extended his stay for fourteen days.

On 12 June, Cohn-Bendit with other student leaders trooped into the BBC studio to record the filmed documentary *Students in Revolt*. Shown on BBC1 (13 June), it proved something of a damp squib. With Cohn-Bendit were eleven other students, and together their garbled mix of opinion and dialectic resulted in a muddle of voices and ideas about student unrest and society in general. The *Guardian* critic Stanley Reynolds called Cohn-Bendit's contribution 'unclear and vague'. Milton Shulman in the London *Evening Standard* described Cohn-Bendit as 'this chubby left-wing ogre'. The House of Commons debated, and deplored, the visit of the German agitator, who spent the day visiting the London School of Economics.

Danny Cohn-Bendit left the UK for France on 15 June. And that was about it for British student protest in 1968. Bristol students staged a 'sleep-in' on 17 June, but the academic year was almost over, and everyone was dispersing to their vacation jobs. The government breathed a sigh of relief. From November, Mrs Hart could be safely left to deal with any more 'youth' problems.

By contrast, West Germany was gaining a reputation for extremist 'youth' violence with political overtones. In April, a revolutionary-minded student leader named Rudi Dutschke was shot in the head by an anti-Communist, but survived and moved to Britain to recover (he was later offered a place at Cambridge University), only to be expelled in 1971 as an 'undesirable alien'. That same month, a militant named Andreas Baader, associated with a left-wing group known as the Red Army Faction, had started fires in two department stores in Frankfurt, in protest against the Vietnam War. Baader and his three companions in arson were quickly arrested. It was the start of a noteworthy terrorist career. Baader and his girlfriend Gudrun Esslin became heroes of the radical underground, until Baader was caught speeding in a car and rearrested. This time he escaped, with the help of fellow radical Ulrike Meinhof, in a farcical jailbreak. Meinhof had persuaded the prison authorities to let her interview Baader in a Berlin library, under the pretext of setting up a book deal. During the interview, she and two other women accomplices let in a masked gunman; the women also produced guns, a librarian was shot, and all four plus Baader got away through a window.

For a time, the Baader-Meinhof gang was notorious, and the Red Army Faction one of Europe's most dangerous terrorist groups. Baader was caught in 1972, and he and Gudrun Esslin died in prison in 1977. The official verdict was suicide. Ulrike Meinhof was found dead in a car in 1976.

Such violent activities had few echoes in Britain. The government felt it could relax. The minister of youth could concentrate on more important duties as government Paymaster General. And if you didn't have a revolution, you could always sing about it, like John Lennon. The Rolling Stones also wrote a 'revolutionary' song, 'Street Fighting Man', released in 1968.

It was at this time that a young man named John Major returned to Britain, after working for a bank in Nigeria. Having left school at 16, he took work with Standard Bank, then returned from Africa in 1968 to pursue some kind of career. Within three years he had been selected as a parliamentary candidate, and by 1974 he was in the Commons as a Conservative MP. He was on the road that in 1990 would lead to Downing Street.

Gender politics

On 7 June 1968 women workers at Ford in Dagenham went on strike. This in itself seemed no big deal. The women were sewing machinists who made covers for car seats. The cause of their unrest was unequal pay. As part of a Ford rearrangement, their job was being reclassified as Category B ('less skilled') instead of Category C ('more skilled'). They also learnt that their pay would be 15 per cent less than that received by men on the B rate. Women machinists at Ford's Hailwood plant on Merseyside later joined the strike.

With no car seat covers, Ford found its assembly line stitched up, as all car production at Dagenham and Hailwood was briefly halted. Into the industrial battlefield strode the recently appointed secretary of state for employment and productivity, Barbara Castle. Her intervention brought an end to the strike after three weeks, and a deal the following year, giving the women the same Category B rate as men. But the women's sense of injustice at being labelled 'less skilled' endured, and was not resolved until fuller strike action in 1984.

The machinists' strike inspired, the following year, the formation of the National Joint Action Campaign Committee for Women's Equal Rights (even the acronym was a mouthful: NJACCWER), and in 1970 the passing of the

Equal Pay Act, which for the first time in Britain set out to equalise the pay and employment conditions of men and women.

Barbara Castle was Britain's most prominent woman politician in 1968. There were other women ministers, including Judith Hart, Jennie Lee and Shirley Williams, but Castle was the most senior. In 1964 when Labour took power, she had been only the fourth woman to hold a Cabinet position, as the first minister for overseas development. MP for Blackburn since the Labour landslide of 1945, Mrs Castle (born Barbara Betts on 6 October 1910), had attracted further public interest as minister of transport (1965–68) when, a non-driver herself, she had introduced the breathalyser and made permanent the 70mph (112km/h) speed limit. She also brought in legislation to ensure all new cars had seat belts.

In April 1968 Harold Wilson promoted the flame-haired and often volatile Barbara Castle to first secretary of state, in charge of employment and productivity. Her intervention in the Dagenham women's strike was one of her first actions in the new role, but she was to plunge into far greater controversy within a year, when in 1969 she introduced a government White Paper containing proposals aimed at cutting the power of the trade unions. The White Paper, 'In Place of Strife', was to cause a Cabinet row, threats of resignation and accusations from Castle's critics of a betrayal of socialist principles. The row dented Labour unity; it was blamed or at least held partly responsible by some for Labour's defeat in the 1970 general election. The White Paper never matured into legislation. The ructions over 'In Place of Strife' brought to a head the political disagreements between Barbara Castle and her Cabinet colleague James Callaghan. Political enmities are rarely completely forgotten, and when Callaghan succeeded Wilson as prime minister in 1976, he at once sacked Barbara Castle, by then in charge of health and social services. She later told an interviewer that Callaghan had justified her removal by saying the Cabinet needed younger members. She said that remark occasioned her most restrained moment in political life, when she refrained from biting back with, 'Then why not start with yourself, Jim?'

Sixties feminism, sometimes known as 'second wave feminism' because it succeeded the suffragist campaign of the late nineteenth and early twentieth centuries, was gathering impetus by 1968. Many of the driving issues came from the United States, where feminists such as Betty Friedan, author of

The Feminine Mystique (1963), had linked the feminist movement to major campaigns for equal pay, civil rights and abortion rights. Typical of the changing mood were a growing number of feminist books and magazines to spread the message and exchange ideas, such as *No More Miss America*, a 1968 press release for the Redstockings Group, Mary Daly's *The Church and the Second Sex*, Kate Millett's *Sexual Politics* and indignant feminist reactions to questions such as 'What Sort of Man Reads *Playboy*?' (a 1968 ad-line – answer: 'a can-do young guy with an eye on the top job ...'). Britain's best-known feminist publisher Virago would make its debut very soon, in 1973, and the Church of Scotland had decided it could ordain women.

The Bobby Kennedy killing

Martin Luther King Jr's assassination came at the start of a long, hot summer of unrest and agony in the United States. After the King killing, riots broke out. Anti-Vietnam War protests fuelled student unrest, city ghettos were simmering, and politics was in turmoil with the decision of President Lyndon B. Johnson not to seek a second term. Prospective candidates were on the stump around the country, and one of the most favoured was Bobby Kennedy.

Robert Kennedy had been both his older brother's campaign adviser and Attorney General in the JFK/Johnson administration, before resigning from government in 1964 to run for the Senate. He was now US Senator for New York, darling of the liberal Democratic Party establishment, and regarded by many as the next president – should he choose to run, rather than give way to the vice president and presidential hopeful, Hubert Humphrey, or the radical student-wowing leftist and anti-war candidate Eugene McCarthy.

Kennedy was assumed to have the 'black vote' for his earlier work on civil rights issues, and he had the charisma the other candidates lacked. Few, other than the most optimistic Republicans, doubted that in a Kennedy-Nixon rerun for the presidency in 1968 the younger Kennedy would win.

Kennedy had gone to California to celebrate victory in the Democratic primary, and was poised to receive the Democratic nomination. He had entered the presidential race in March, about three weeks before the King shooting. Voters in the New Hampshire primary had already given the sitting president a bloody nose, awarding outsider Eugene McCarthy 42 per cent of the vote to the president's 49 per cent – this clear evidence of his unpopularity must have weighed on Johnson's mind before he announced he would not run again in 1968. The way was clear for Bobby Kennedy to make his challenge, though he still trailed Humphrey in secured delegates by the time of the California primary (4 June). California gave him victory. His supporters were in buoyant mood as they gathered in the Embassy Room at Los Angeles' Ambassador Hotel just after midnight on 5 June.

Surrounded by cheering supporters, Kennedy's security was minimal: one former FBI agent and two ex-athletes, decathlete Rafer Johnson and footballer Rosey Grier. On his way to speak to reporters, Kennedy was led along a kitchen corridor, shaking hands with wellwishers as he was ushered through the melee. His killer appeared from beside an ice machine. He was holding a rolled-up poster. Hidden inside was a .22 revolver.

As Kennedy was pushed through the throng, the man produced his gun, fired several shots at close range, then was dragged to the ground by the Kennedy entourage. The shots floored Kennedy and wounded bystanders. The presidential candidate was fatally wounded by a bullet entering the brain from very close range.

The attacker, Sirhan Sirhan, was overpowered, though at one point he grabbed the now empty gun again. Kennedy was still conscious, able to ask if everything was OK, and seemingly able to recognise his wife Ethel. But shortly afterwards he fell unconscious, and despite surgery at the City's Hospital of the Good Samaritan he died at 1.44 in the morning of 6 June, more than twenty-four hours after the shooting. He was 42.

Sirhan Sirhan's motive for the killing has been extensively analysed. Born in Jerusalem, he told questioners that his hatred for Kennedy was fired by Kennedy's support for Israel. He had chosen the date (5 June) as the anniversary of the start of the 1967 Six Day War between Israel and neighbouring Arab states. His lawyer argued psychological problems and diminished responsibility, while at one point the accused tried to plead guilty. In 1969 he was convicted of murder and sentenced to life imprisonment in 1972.

At the time of writing he remains in prison, having been denied parole fifteen times. In 2016 he told a parole board he had no memory of shooting

Bobby Kennedy, but could recall only being in the hotel, going to his car, and realising he had drunk too much. He could deny or confirm nothing: he couldn't confess anything because 'it's all vague now'.

Bystander Paul Schrade, a union official and Kennedy campaign organiser in 1968, later testified at Sirhan's fifteenth parole hearing, saying he forgave him. Aged 91 when speaking at the hearing in 2016, Schrade said he believed that an unidentified 'second shooter' had killed Kennedy. His version was that four bullets had been fired from behind the victim, whereas Sirhan was in front of Kennedy, and only fired two aimed shots (one of which hit Schrade) before being tackled, letting off his remaining shots wildly.

For many, Sirhan Sirhan was never a satisfactory Bobby Kennedy assassin, any more than sceptics could accept Lee Harvey Oswald as the lone gunman who shot President Kennedy in 1963. As with the 1968 gunshots, linked to the suggestion of a second gunman, despite subsequent re-examination of testimonies suggesting little real evidence for this theory. Analyses of sound recordings have also been cited, to suggest as many as thirteen shots: Sirhan's pistol held only eight rounds, but this scenario again is disputed.

More far-fetched is the suggestion that Sirhan had been 'brainwashed' into killing Kennedy, using psychological programming that left him with no conscious recollection of his actions.

'Alternative gunman' theories include the allegation that a woman in a polka-dot dress was seen with a man in and around the hotel before the killing and afterwards seen running and actually shouting 'we shot him'. This story was debunked when the alleged witness withdrew the account, a retraction that conspiracy theorists attribute to intimidation of the witness by the CIA. The CIA or the Mafia, or both together, have frequently been suggested as dark forces behind both the King and Kennedy killings.

As Attorney General, Bobby Kennedy had gone to war against organised crime in America. At the same time there were whispers about secretive links between the Kennedy political machine and the mob – John Kennedy, after all, shared a mistress with mob boss Sam Giancana (though not at the same time). Bobby Kennedy had launched a high-profile anti-crime war against the Teamsters union boss Jimmy Hoffa, who was jailed the year before Kennedy was killed. Hoffa was later granted a pardon by President Nixon, was released in 1971 and disappeared in 1975, after visiting a Detroit restaurant to meet two Mafia bosses. Never seen again, he was declared legally dead in 1982. The Hoffa case remains open. Sirhan Sirhan remains in prison.

The lad from East Cheam bows out

Tony Hancock was, sadly, past his golden years in 1968, when he ended his own life in a hotel room in Sydney, Australia. Trying to revive a career that had hit the buffers, and fight inner demons, he had left Britain, where he had won millions of fans and become one of the country's most admired comedians, whose frustrated ambition and aspirations in fiction often seemed to mirror his own in real life.

A hard-graft apprenticeship on the boards as a comic 'turn' at London's Windmill Theatre had followed his debut as a wartime member of Ralph Reader's Gang Show. From stand-up stints entertaining the customers in between the static nude displays at the Windmill, Hancock moved into occasional radio, getting a major break in 1951 with appearances in the radio show *Educating Archie*. Archie was the dummy of ventriloquist Peter Brough.

His own show, *Hancock's Half Hour*, began on BBC Radio in 1954. Written by Ray Galton and Alan Simpson, it ran on radio for seven years and from 1956 also brought Hancock to BBC Television. Galton and Simpson created for the show the eponymous comic Hancock; the comedian's real name (Anthony John) gave way to the grandiloquent Anthony Aloysius St John Hancock.

Hancock's persona, as created by Galton and Simpson, was based on self-delusion. The radio/TV Hancock had an unshakeable belief in his own talent, an aspiration to attempt challenges for which he was unsuited, a sentimental belief that things used to be better years ago, that the world was steadily going downhill, and that his outstanding gifts ('a man of my calibre') were not recognised. The radio Hancock was a comic who thought himself a great actor – his character lived shabbily but with pretensions. He had a secretary, Miss Pugh (Hattie Jacques), and two male associates: Bill (Bill Kerr, pilloried as both slow-witted and Australian) and Sid (Sid James, a chancer liable to inveigle the gullible and idealistic Hancock into money-making schemes or minor scams and disasters). The other permanent fixture in the early shows was Kenneth Williams, popping up in unlikely places and urging everyone to 'stop messing about'. The early radio Hancock had girlfriends (Moira Lister, Andrée Melly); in the later TV incarnation he was a somewhat mournful, sour and lonely bachelor, resident at 23 Railway Cuttings, East Cheam, with pipe dreams of the better life his station deserved. On television, the cast was reduced to 'Hancock' and 'Sid' with occasional appearances from the charlady, Mrs Cravatte (Patricia Hayes).

By the mid-1960s Hancock had gone solo. In 1960 he had starred in a film, *The Rebel*, the story of an office worker who goes to Paris to become an artist. In 1961, he ended his TV partnership with long-time scriptwriters Galton and Simpson, who went away to devise *Steptoe and Son*.

Hancock made a second film, *The Punch and Judy Man* (1962), about a struggling seaside entertainer. He then switched channels, leaving the BBC for ATV, but his commercial television series failed to recapture the brilliance of his earlier work. TV appearances continued until 1967, though by now heavy drinking and unreliability were affecting his performances. His private life was also complicated. Married in 1950, he had a long affair with his publicist Freddie Ross, whom he married in 1965 after divorcing his wife Cicely. At the same time he was in a relationship with Joan Malin, wife of actor John le Mesurier. In 1965, Freddie attempted to kill herself.

Hancock was not in a particularly good state, after a poorly received series for ATV, when invited to make a series in Australia for the Seven Network. He flew out to Australia in March 1968, but completed only three of thirteen scheduled episodes of *Hancock Down Under*.

On 25 June 1968, Tony Hancock's body was found in an apartment he had rented in Sydney. He had drunk a bottle of vodka and taken pills, leaving a suicide note in which he wrote that 'things seem to go wrong too many times'.

Since 1968, Tony Hancock's comedy has continued to attract new and old fans. Moody introspection seems to chime across the generations. His best friend, John Le Mesurier, began his service as the long-suffering Sergeant Wilson in *Dad's Army* a month after Hancock died. Hancock believed, like 'the lad himself', that he was better than those around him. He could dispense with his scriptwriters, his 'support' (Sid, Bill, Hattie, Kenneth Williams and the rest) and go it alone. Even more galling perhaps was to realise that they could all get on pretty well without him. Hancock's films were not as successful as he hoped, while Sid James became the mainstay of successive *Carry On* films. Galton and Simpson no longer needed him: they were enjoying plaudits and ratings success with *Steptoe and Son*. The Australia series was to play on his established small-screen persona; the would-be Shakespearean stage strutter from East Cheam was to collide with Australian no-nonsense realism. But Hancock's self-belief had gone; he presumably thought there would be no second series of his Australian show. Evidently, the planners had decided it was worth a try; most of the crew knew, but not Hancock.

As he might have said, 'Stone me, what a life.'

7

July

THE PROFESSIONAL APPROACH

Paying the game?

Vince Lombardi, retiring head coach of the US Super Bowl-winning Green Bay Packers, believed sport was simple. It was about winning. His many dicta included the ultra-professional view that 'winning isn't everything – it's the only thing'. It was such professionalism that brought Leeds United two football trophies in 1968, the Inter-Cities Fairs Cup and the English League Cup. A scruffy 1–0 win against Arsenal in a League Cup final at Wembley was memorable only for fans of Don Revie's Leeds side – then one of the most consistent, yet most often criticised football teams in the country. Leeds' crime was to be too professional, which equated to boring, or clinical, or both. Yet the Leeds side was rich in talent, with a gifted manager in Revie, who won the First Division title in 1969 and later managed England. But for all his achievements, Revie never quite won the same affection and respect accorded to the likes of Matt Busby, Bill Shankly, Bill Nicholson, or Alf Ramsey. Although the English and Scottish leagues were professional, amateur soccer still flourished. The 1968 FA Amateur Cup Final was won by Leytonstone, who beat Chesham United 1–0; but the last all-amateur final was only six years away, as professionalism, albeit often part-time, took over.

Professionalism in sport was still regarded with suspicion, even disfavour, by some amateur administrators. Athletics was supposedly amateur, as was Rugby Union. So was tennis. Pro tennis had been around for years, confined to a small circuit of players, including ex-amateur champions, playing what amounted to exhibition matches. The major tournaments (US, French, Australian, Wimbledon) were firmly amateur-only. Prizes were awarded but winners took away trophies, not eye-watering cheques. Sponsors had prowled around the gates of Wimbledon, Forest Hills and the other temples of tennis, looking for a way in, but until 1968 'big money' had been kept out. If a player wanted a career in tennis, he or she might become a coach, but having turned pro they could no longer compete at Wimbledon. Former champions such as Jack Kramer, Frank Sedgman and Lew Hoad had turned professional, but after making the move they were for years barred from walking onto Wimbledon's Centre Court again. The latest examples included Rod Laver, who had turned professional in 1962. In 1967 he won the first professional tournament to be staged at Wimbledon.

In fact, Wimbledon, often seen as epitomising blazered stuffiness, was thinking radically. Having let the professionals in to play on its hallowed lawns, in 1968 it now wanted to go further and stage the first 'Open' tournament. In December 1967, the British Lawn Tennis Association took the bold step to end the distinction between amateur and professional; the 1968 All England Lawn Tennis Championships at Wimbledon would be open to all. The International Lawn Tennis Federation (ILTF) in a fit of righteous indignation briefly expelled the British, but soon retracted; the winds of change were as irresistibly strong in sport as in world politics, sweetened by the financial inducements of broadcasters and sponsors, who saw open tennis as an attractive new product. In March 1968, the ILTF rescinded its opposition, agreeing in principle to open tennis. The French Championships, first major event of the year, started the open era; fittingly, an all-Australian 'ex-pro' final saw Ken Rosewall beat Laver.

So when the crowds flocked to Wimbledon that summer, they came in hope of seeing once more old favourites returned from pro pastures, not only Rosewall and Laver, but Pancho Gonzales, a professional since 1949. Laver returned to Centre Court with undimmed brilliance to win his third Wimbledon men's title in just over an hour, at the expense of fellow Australian Tony Roche. The men's doubles produced an epic battle, as Roche and John Newcombe beat Rosewall and Fred Stolle in a marathon five-setter. The women's singles also had a champion of rare quality and grit: Billie Jean King of the USA, who took the title for the third year running. Laver's prize money was £2,000 (a pittance by modern standards); for winning the women's title, Billie Jean King took away just £750.

Across the Atlantic, Britain had a winner too, in Virginia Wade. She had won the first open event staged in Britain, the Hard Court Championship at Bournemouth, but as an amateur refused the cash prize. She then turned professional and won the first United States Open. The 1968 US Championships at Forest Hills were also notable for the first African-American men's champion, Arthur Ashe, then still an officer in the US Army.

Professionalism existed across the sports. Lester Piggott, most professional and focused of jockeys, won the 1968 Derby on Sir Ivor. Gary Player of South Africa won the Open golf title at Carnoustie, the second of his three Open titles. In cricket, Yorkshire claimed a third successive county championship, as yet disdaining to follow other counties in signing overseas stars. Imported cricketers were having a greater impact on English cricket, as counties were allowed to sign one foreign player without residential qualification. Batsmen were the most eagerly sought, players of the calibre of Barry Richards (South Africa), Rohan Kanhai (West Indies) and the incomparable Gary Sobers (also West Indies), whose 36 runs in an over for Nottinghamshire against Glamorgan sent him yet again into the record books. An amateur of the old school, Colin Cowdrey, played his 100th Test match for England in July against Australia, and in so doing became the first cricketer to make a century of international appearances.

Nuclear matters

On 1 July 1968 an agreement between the three major nuclear powers (the United States, the Soviet Union and the United Kingdom) was an important step towards preventing the spread of nuclear weapons to other states. The Treaty on the Non-Proliferation of Nuclear Weapons had sixty-two signatories in all, the three nuclear powers agreeing not to help other nations obtain or manufacture nuclear weapons. The treaty that became effective from March 1970 remains in force, though not every country has signed it. The treaty was a qualified 'disarmament' agreement; it obliged non-nuclear states to refrain from building nuclear weapons, yet allowed nations that already had 'the bomb' to retain their nuclear arsenals. The 1968 agreement embodied the understanding that the nuclear powers would be prepared to assist other nations in developing nuclear power for peaceful, civilian purposes – suggesting a distinction between military and civilian nuclear science that was considerably less than clear-cut.

Nuclear issues were seldom out of the news. The French H-bomb test on 23 August 1968 was condemned by peace campaigners. France had developed its nuclear and thermonuclear weapons independently. In 1958, De Gaulle vetoed any French participation in a proposed 'Euro-bomb' programme in collaboration with West Germany and Italy, a suggestion aired after the creation in 1957 of Euratom (the European Atomic Energy Community). The latest French nuclear test, code-named Canopus, took place in French Polynesia. Its 'success' made France the fifth nation to test a hydrogen bomb. De Gaulle insisted France must have an independent nuclear deterrent, not one dependent (like Britain's) on US-supplied missiles. The French programme required a diverse delivery system, with strategic bombers such as the Mirage III and IV, land-based ballistic missiles, and submarine-launched missiles similar to the US Polaris. Accordingly, the French Navy in 1968 awaited its first missile submarine, then being built and due in 1971.

Britain's first nuclear missile-armed submarine was already at sea – the culmination of a long and often painful process in reshaping the country's nuclear deterrent. Post-war Britain had been obliged to develop its nuclear deterrent independently, but in fairly close collaboration with the Americans in some areas. Like France, Britain had developed and tested its own nuclear weapons, and British bomb tests through the 1950s had led to the development of a weapon suitable for the RAF's bomber force. A coherent policy was often hard to discern. The RAF had been given three types of nuclear bombers in the 1950s, the 'V-bomber' force (Valiants, Victors and Vulcans). Surely one would have sufficed? In 1960, the U-2 incident, in which a US spy plane was shot down over the Soviet Union, had demonstrated the effectiveness of missile air-defence systems. Any high-flying aircraft was almost certain to be shot down. Unless they could sneak in at low level, beneath the radar, the RAF's bombers had little realistic hope of reaching their targets.

The British had therefore considered a land-based intercontinental ballistic missile (ICBM), but Blue Streak had been abandoned in 1960 as too expensive and too vulnerable. The Macmillan government then approached the Americans to buy Skybolt, an air-launched missile that could be fitted to the V-bombers. The Skybolt deal had come to grief in 1962, after the missile's failure to reach expectations, and the United States had opted for a submarine-launched missile system: Polaris.

Macmillan and President Kennedy had agreed a deal in 1963. Britain would buy the US missile, but build its own submarines. British officials had apparently been startled by the generosity of the US offer, which took into account Britain's insistence on maintaining an independent nuclear deterrent. Labour had also signed off the deal, though Labour supporters included unilateral disarmers and CND members. The party had committed to an independent deterrent, and the Labour Government gaining power in 1964 had continued with Polaris, but cut the number of missile-submarines from five to four: *Resolution*, *Repulse*, *Renown*, and *Revenge*.

The submarines were built by Vickers-Armstrong in Barrow and Cammell Laird at Birkenhead, though the missile compartment was US-made, as were the Polaris missiles themselves. The warheads were British. Each submarine could carry sixteen Polaris A3 missiles, the weapon's third generation since the first test firing in 1960. The 1968 version A3 had a range of 4,600km (2,500 nautical miles). HMS *Resolution* was the first Royal Navy Polaris submarine to go to sea, in 1966, and on 15 February 1968 it successfully test fired a Polaris missile from the test range off the east coast of the United States. In June 1968, *Resolution* was ready to go on patrol. That the missile submarines were all named after historic battleships showed they were now the Royal Navy's capital ships. Polaris remained in service until 1994, when the first submarines armed with the new Trident missile left on their long, secretive submerged patrols.

The RAF felt keenly the loss of its nuclear deterrent role. By 1968 the Vulcan bomber, still in squadron service, had been redeployed from high altitude to low-level penetration, and the Victor bombers had been converted to flying fuel tankers. As the Royal Navy sent its first missile-carrying submarine to sea, the RAF was concerned that it had lost both strategic and tactical primacy, with the demotion of the V-bombers, and the cancellation of the TSR-2 aircraft in April 1965. So there were muted celebrations in 1968 to commemorate the Royal Air Force's 50th anniversary. The service had been founded in 1918, bringing together the Royal Flying Corps and the Royal Naval Air Service. Top brass and lower ranks had new command structure changes to absorb. In April 1968, RAF Bomber and Fighter Commands were combined into Strike Command; Coastal Command was subsumed into the new arrangement later that year.

To fill the gap in the RAF's inventory, the government in 1967 had ordered fifty F-111 aircraft from the United States, in a British variant, but in January 1968 it cancelled the order. US Phantoms were purchased instead, and the RAF received its first US-built Phantom in August 1968. Longer term, the RAF would have to wait for Anglo-French projects still on the drawing board, which eventually emerged as the Jaguar and Tornado; in the interim, pilots had the supersonic Lightning, but too many other aircraft of 1950s vintage or earlier, no longer competitive with the best in the world. However, hovering just over the horizon was something new: a truly revolutionary aircraft, the Harrier 'jump jet'. It was already demonstrating its unique capabilities as the world's first VTOL (Vertical Take-Off and Landing) combat aircraft. The first Harrier would be delivered for pilot conversion training early in 1969.

Around the world in 354 days

Lone yachtsmen were very much a 1960s thing. Francis Chichester (1901–72) had captured headlines in 1967, completing a single-handed voyage around the globe in a day over nine months. Chichester had attained international celebrity for his voyage in *Gipsy Moth IV*, at the age of 65, having first attracted public notice by winning the initial solo transatlantic yacht race in 1960. Another keen middle-aged sailor, Alec Rose (1908–91), had sailed in the second Atlantic race held in 1964. A former Royal Navy mechanic, who during the Second World War had served on a sloop escorting convoys, Rose was no stranger to rough water and ocean storms,

After the war, Alec Rose had taken up sailing as recreation – his 'day job' being a nurseryman and greengrocer. In 1967, he had hoped to sail around the world at the same time as Chichester. He had a boat, a second-hand converted ketch originally built in India, named *Lively Lady*. Unfortunately, mechanical problems and a collision had put *Lively Lady* in dock, so Alec Rose had to bide his time, listening to the news reports as Chichester set out on his lone voyage. Rose was still preparing for his own departure when Chichester returned to a hero's welcome in May 1967. In July, Chichester was knighted by the Queen at Greenwich.

As the cheers died away and cameras flashed, Alec Rose, without fanfare, was putting out to sea, leaving his wife Dorothy to supervise the fruit and veg business and trace on the map how her lone voyager was faring.

Like Chichester, Rose headed for a stopover in Australia, arriving in Melbourne after 155 days at sea. His arrival made news and attracted a large crowd, including Australian Prime Minister Harold Holt. Later that day, Sunday 17 December 1967, Holt went for a swim on a favourite beach and disappeared, never to be seen again. While the Australians began an inquiry into their missing premier and selected his replacement, Alec Rose sailed on. Not intending to re-enter a port again, he was obliged to do so in New Zealand, stopping off to repair a damaged mast.

Before the days of GPS satellites and internet links to provide regular updates on sailors crossing the remote southern ocean, Alec Rose's progress was at times unknown. It was from one radio report to the next that his boat's course was tracked. Appetite for news of lone sailors was still keen; media expectations were high as *Lively Lady* was spotted heading back up the English Channel, to receive a warm welcome when she entered harbour at Southsea (Portsmouth) on 4 July 1968. Alec Rose had come home, ten days before his 60th birthday.

Like Chichester, Alec Rose was honoured with a knighthood. Always a quiet, modest and rather shy man, he observed in the book about his exploit that he had always been a loner, with an abiding love for the sea in all its moods. *Lively Lady* outlived him; lovingly maintained and rebuilt to give sail training adventures to young people, she remains at Portsmouth, the port from which so many of Britain's greatest maritime exploits have begun.

8

August

FREE FOR ALL

The Troubles begin

Did Northern Ireland's Troubles begin in August 1968? It seemed so, though the history of Northern Ireland since 1921, when the island of Ireland was partitioned, had seldom been without tension, mainly between its Catholic and Protestant communities. These tensions had been largely forgotten by people on the mainland in the 1960s, when so-called religious or nationalist quarrels seemed relics from history. Then in August 1968 'the Troubles' flared up again, and 'civil rights' became a front-page issue in the United Kingdom.

Catholics in Northern Ireland were a minority in a province run by Unionist/Loyalist Protestants. In 1967, the Northern Ireland Civil Rights Association (NICRA) had been formed in Belfast with a mission to campaign for Catholic communities. These communities, with their own distinct geographies, were regarded by many hardline Unionists as 'the other side' in religion and politics, 'Catholic' equating to 'nationalist'. For many years since 1921, Unionists had slewed voting rights in local elections and public housing allocation, so that Catholics claimed to suffer widespread discrimination, and especially in employment.

Civil rights campaigners were also keen to see the end of the Ulster Special Constabulary, the hated 'B-Specials', an auxiliary, all-Protestant paramilitary police reserve force widely blamed for unlawful actions. The Ulster Government, led by Terence O'Neill, appeared resistant to any move towards real reform, in the face of trenchant and vocal opposition from extremist Unionists such as Ian Paisley's Ulster Protestant Action organisation. The mild-mannered O'Neill was a target for all sides; he had eggs thrown at him by Protestants.

Small-scale protests had been rumbling all year – for example, the Derry Housing Action Committee's sit-down demonstrations against housing discrimination. But with August, and the 'marching season' for Protestant Orangemen, the temperature rose. On 24 August 1968, NICRA staged the first 'civil rights' march in Northern Ireland, a modest event from Coalisland to Dungannon. Among the marchers was Belfast student Bernadette Devlin, who the following year would be elected an MP. The marchers' mood was initially cheerful, until police barred their way into the town of Dungannon, their intended destination, but on the whole the march passed off peacefully.

In October, the Derry Housing Action Committee planned to hold a second a march in Londonderry. The Apprentice Boys of Derry, loudly and fiercely Protestant and Unionist, announced they would rally on the same day, in effect compelling the Northern Ireland Government to ban all parades. This it did on 3 October, but on 5 October the civil rights march went ahead anyway. The Royal Ulster Constabulary (RUC) came out in force, as did the TV cameras. And the TV pictures were dramatic and shocking. They showed marchers being baton-charged by police, along with live footage of water cannon, petrol bombs and bonfires. The many casualties included Labour MP Gerry Fitt, who spoke afterwards of the RUC's 'stormtrooper tactics' – a charge rejected by Northern Ireland's home affairs minister William Craig.

For viewers in the rest of the UK, coverage of the Derry march and the street violence came as a revelation. In Northern Ireland unrest spread, particularly among students at Queen's University Belfast where a protest against the RUC brought out hundreds of students in a sit-down demonstration. Some tried to take over the parliament building at Stormont, claiming the student unrest at the Sorbonne in Paris as their inspiration.

On 4 November Harold Wilson, having discussed the crisis with Irish Taoiseach (premier) Jack Lynch, summoned O'Neill to London and warned him that unless order was restored, the British Government would have to intervene. On 13 November, Craig banned all marches except 'customary' parades – which in effect meant Loyalist ones. O'Neill responded to the pressure on 22 November with the offer of a five-point reform package. He sacked Craig and on 9 December made a TV plea for breathing space, asking for calm and more time to institute changes.

It was not to be. 1969 would see more demonstrations and counter-demonstrations, and a request by the Northern Ireland administration for the British Army to restore order. What began as an intended short-term deployment of a few British soldiers (at first welcomed by the Catholic/Nationalist protesters) became a bitter, bloody and divisive commitment lasting from 1969 until 2007.

The Prague Spring withers

While US and Western European minds, certainly liberal minds, were preoccupied with the war in Vietnam, the Soviet Union's rulers felt free to be as illiberal as they liked with their East European fiefdom. When the Czechs stirred and showed they wanted reform, Moscow did what it had done in Hungary in 1956 – sent in the tanks.

It was all done in the name of Warsaw Pact unity. Bulgaria, Hungary and Poland sent troops to assist their comrades in the Red Army. Romania and Albania were less dutiful in solidarity, but the East German leadership was, as ever, doglike in its keenness to demonstrate what good Communists they were, and stood ready to commit East German soldiers across the border – until the message from Moscow bluntly told them to stay on their side. Moscow did not want to be seen sanctioning another Czech invasion by Germany, no matter what the justification.

The so-called Prague Spring of 1968 had its origins in economic stagnation and intellectual indignation. The Czech economy, one of the most industrialised in Eastern Europe before 1945, had fared poorly under the rigid rule making and quota setting of Soviet-style planning. Attempts at restructuring the economy had begun under Antonín Novotný, president from 1957 and general secretary of the local Czech Communist Party. An old-style hardliner, this former blacksmith and Nazi concentration camp prisoner had little time for Czechoslovakia's liberal elite, which included film directors such as Miloš Forman and writers such as Milan Kundera and the young Václav Havel. Their work was often subtly or blatantly critical of Communist authoritarianism. Novotný had little to fear from opponents until the autumn of 1967, when he was challenged by a Slovak reformer, Alexander Dubček. Students took to the streets of Prague to back Dubček, making Novotný so nervous that he asked Moscow what he should do. A visit to Prague by Soviet leader Leonid Brezhnev proved disappointing: Brezhnev told Novotný he had to solve his own problems.

This Novotný signally failed to do. In January 1968, the Communist leadership in Czechoslovakia chose Dubček to replace Novotný as first secretary and began an energetic campaign to oust old-style 'Stalinists' from positions of authority in the trade union and youth organisations.

On 22 March 1968, Novotný realised his time was up. He assigned the presidency to an army leader, General Ludvík Svoboda, who signified he would not oppose change. So Dubček appeared to have a free hand – or at least a freer one – and he embarked on a programme of reform. Censorship was lifted; newspapers, radio and television were instructed to promulgate the new, freer-thinking attitudes. A new democratic party was taking embryonic shape, with plans made for a liberating 14th Party Congress in September. An action programme boldly used the terms 'democracy' and 'nationalism' to suggest that the Czechs should work out their own form of socialism, with a federal system to take account of the country's two main geographical regions: Slovakia and Bohemia.

The genie was out of the bottle. Newspapers began to publish material that was clearly anti-Soviet, yet all this was happening under the very real shadow of Soviet military power. Warsaw Pact troops were actually inside the country, on manoeuvres in Czechoslovakia in June. And in July the rattled Soviet leaders called on the Eastern bloc allies to discuss the situation. The Czechs were first excluded from the meeting, then summoned like errant schoolboys before the stern gaze of headmaster Comrade Brezhnev. Where his predecessor Khrushchev had guffawed and bullied, Leonid Brezhnev simply clenched his eyebrows and looked more grimly sepulchral. His senior co-ruler in the Kremlin, Alexsei Kosygin, invariably looked as if he'd eaten a bad oyster, and for these Cold War dinosaurs, the Czech spring was gut-achingly bad news.

While the Warsaw Pact loyalty club members dutifully tut-tutted about the dangers of revisionism and counter-revolution, the Czech capital Prague was enjoying an extended springtime of liberal-sounding ideas. Democracy can be a heady brew. Freed from Novotný's heavy hand, the Czech freedom bars were open all hours, with the usual suspects (writers, academics, students) eager to expose the iniquities of the past, including the usual brutal and nasty hardline stuff – persecution, purges, show trials, arbitrary imprisonment, disappearances. The reformers were full of plans for a brighter social-democratic future. Printing presses ran out thousands of copies of eagerly read periodicals and pamphlets; the radio was full of freedom chatter and passionate argument.

Dubček, still a Communist, albeit a reform-minded one, knew he was walking a tightrope, teetering across a bear pit with an increasingly grumpy Russian bear sharpening its claws beneath him. His new programme called for the anticipated freedoms (press, speech, movement), for more consumer goods in the shops, and for keeping the secret police out of sight, if not wholly out of action. Dubček and his inner circle were rightly nervous of going too far; they might denounce, but were hesitant about overturning the old familiar regime in favour of the 'bourgeois democracy' so despised by Communist hardliners. Such caution was not, of course, to the liking of the more excitable, caught up in Prague's spring fever. No more conservative timidity; they wanted action, and revolution-minded students sought to draw industrial workers into the new movement.

Inside the Kremlin, the mood darkened as Brezhnev grew ever more thunderous and menacing. He knew that while Dubček had some support from within the Warsaw Pact (the Romanians were, as ever, troublesome), there were those inside the Czech Communist Party ready to toe the Kremlin line. Romania's leader Nicolae Ceauşescu was refusing to back any Warsaw Pact action, and even went to Prague to demonstrate his support for Dubček. The Russians were not amused, but knew they could rely on the Poles, Hungarians and East Germans.

The presence of Warsaw Pact forces in and around the embattled Czechs gave Moscow a massive edge. In a pacific gesture, the Kremlin said it was ready to pull back troops, provided the Czechs kept their house in order. On 3 August, Moscow's dutiful allies issued a declaration at Bratislava, pledging loyalty to the principles of Marxism–Leninism and a determination to defeat bourgeois ideology. Where such ideology seemed to be gaining ground in a Warsaw Pact country, intervention would be guaranteed to protect the people.

Intervention to protect the people meant crushing the reform movement. On 20–21 August 1968 troops from five Warsaw Pact states moved into Czechoslovakia. An estimated 200,000 soldiers and around 2,000 tanks crossed the border. There was little resistance from the Czech Army, shut up inside its bases. There was more resistance from Czech and Slovak civilians. More than seventy people were killed, and almost 300 badly wounded in street battles. Crowds poured onto city streets to confront the tanks. It was like Hungary in 1956 all over again, and just as hopeless.

Dubček was arrested and whisked away to Moscow along with President Svoboda and other Czech leaders. International reaction was muted, at least at government level. Britain, the United States and other free nations called for a meeting of the UN Security Council. The Czech ambassador to the UN condemned the aggression, to which the Soviet ambassador replied that all his country had done was provide 'fraternal assistance'. Newly appointed US ambassador to Prague was Shirley Temple Black, (the former Hollywood child star); she reported seeing tanks in the street, and people firing from windows. Reports spoke of arrests and a security crackdown, with protesters shot. Czechs with the means to do so fled to the West. Others continued to demonstrate defiance, and the resistance gained a tragic martyr within months, when on 19 January 1969 student Jan Palach burned himself to death in Prague's Wenceslas Square.

Unknown to the public at the time, the British Government even contemplated military intervention should Soviet expansionism become over-ambitious. Such fears apparently reached their height in November 1968, with the Foreign Office nervous of an imminent Soviet move against Romania. Documents from meetings at this time include references to the feasibility of sending special forces to support guerrilla operations, should Russian tanks attack Romania. There were even fears in Whitehall that the Russians might chance their luck by attacking states outside the Warsaw Pact, such as Sweden, Austria and Iran, or take control of the whole of Berlin.

However, the crisis eased. Dubček had been emasculated, but not murdered. He had to agree to toe the line, knowing it was for a short time only, but he was spared the pistol shot. No gulag, no 'disappearance'. He stayed in power, nominally, until April 1969 when he was dismissed as head of the Czech Government, expelled from the party and sent to work as a forestry official. He was replaced by a Kremlin puppet, Gustáv Husák, and most of the 1968 reforms were blown away with the return of winter. One change survived: Dubček's decision to federalise the country into separate republics for Czechs and Slovaks. This happened in 1969. The two socialist republics lasted until 1990 and the second, more permanent, Velvet Revolution, which brought Communist rule in the two republics to an unlamented end.

The last steam train

Britain's last steam train, which waved farewell in 1968, represented the final footnote to Dr Beeching's pruning of Britain's rail network. Dr Richard Beeching ran, or ran down, the nationalised British Railways from 1962 to 1965. His 1964 report, *The Reshaping of British Railways*, set out some unpalatable facts about the uneconomic state of the network. Of 27,000km (17,000 miles) of track, half was underused, carrying just 5 per cent of the railway traffic. Beeching's solution was drastic: close down the underused lines. It was the same story with freight. Of about 2,000 stations handling rail freight, only 100 or so were really productive, handling more than half the total freight carried. The passenger rolling stock was also underused; about 30 per cent of coaches were on the move most of the time, while the remainder were required only in the rush hours or at holiday times.

Beeching's solution was economically logical at the time, but environmentally questionable, socially destructive and, in the longer term, a negative and unimaginative response. He saw the railways as having three main functions: moving commuters in and out of London and the south-east; connecting major cities by intercity express trains; and freightliner services moving containers from a network of thirty road depots. The railways were publicly owned. That cost money. Much of the railway was underused. That meant spending money for hard-to-quantify 'social' benefits. Uneconomic lines were being subsidised. Britain could ill afford it. And more people were turning to the car.

The effects of the cuts were dramatic. Between 1962 and 1970, the number of locomotives on the railways was reduced from over 12,000 to just 4,500. The number of freight wagons was halved to 370,000. The 6,800 stations at the start of the 1960s had dwindled to around 2,800 by the end of the decade, and the overall track length cut from 17,000 to under 12,000 miles (under 19,300km).

Local communities had seen uneconomic lines go, often with regret but with resignation. More people now had cars, so what was the point of a local train chugging between small stations, carrying half a dozen people and a few parcels? Cars were new, shiny and with-it; trains were dirty, rusty, smoky and very unglamorous by comparison. Despite a modernisation programme, British Rail had done little to make railways attractive, or even pleasant. Stations were spartan, much of the rolling stock of creaking pre-war design, steam trains seemed almost Victorian, and while trainspotters might feel excited over a new diesel locomotive, few others found this particular new technology stimulating to the eye or imagination. New motorways made newspaper headlines, new cars caught the eye in weekend colour supplements; the sight of a Deltic diesel locomotive hauling the London to Edinburgh service seemed prosaic by comparison, even if it could top 100mph (160km/h).

The end of steam seemed inevitable, but tears were shed when the last steam trains puffed along British Railways track for the last time. The final regular British passenger train hauled by steam ran on 11 August 1968; it was a special event, and the journey from Liverpool to Carlisle marked the end of daily steam services. Cynics pointed out that British Railways had ceased normal steam operation across the network without fanfare, then realised it could make money from this last hurrah – hence the so-called Fifteen Guinea Special, to draw enthusiasts keen to make the last trip behind steam. The locomotive, *Oliver Cromwell*, a Britannia-class Pacific bearing the number 70013, had been in service since 1951 on the East Anglia Main Line (Norwich–London). Of four locomotives used on that last August 1968 Fifteen Guinea Special, only one (No. 44781) ended up on the scrapheap. The others (Nos 45110, 44871 and 70013 *Oliver Cromwell*) went for preservation. Two coaches used on the 1968 run were also preserved.

The train was thirty-three minutes late into Carlisle, fourteen minutes late on the return trip to Manchester Victoria, and nine minutes late only by the time it got back to Liverpool Lime Street.

While British Railways had finally shunted steam into the sidings, loco buffs were keen to keep steam engines working. Across the country unwanted locomotives were sold or rescued, to be restored and run on heritage railways, using reopened stretches of line – like the Keighley and Worth Railway, which was reopened in 1968, having been closed six years earlier. Such railways continue to provide young and old with a 'steam experience'. And of those who mourned the passing of steam in 1968, few could have predicted that in the next century, Britain would gain a brand-new steam locomotive. No. 60163 *Tornado*, a Peppercorn-class A1, built 1994–2008, was the first mainline steam locomotive built in Britain (and at Darlington, where steam railway history began in the early 1800s) since British Railways' *Evening Star* (1960).

The end of steam and closure of branch lines marked the end, too, for many of Britain's small stations, their fate lamented in a 1964 Flanders and Swann song ('Slow Train' from *At the Drop of Another Hat*). It was farewell to Dog Dyke, Tumby Woodside, Troublehouse Halt, Scholar Green; the end of over a century's service for an idiosyncratic array of stations, station gardens, station masters and station cats. Nostalgic affection for local lines, like the small North Staffordshire Railways (NSR) serving the Potteries area (Stoke-on-Trent) had even contributed to a theatrical success: Peter Cheeseman's play *The Knotty*, a musical documentary about the NSR, which operated as an independent company from its first train in 1848 to its amalgamation with the London, Midland and Scottish (LMS) in 1923.

Somehow, service stations on the new motorways lacked the same appeal as these vanishing railways. Britain's first motorway, the M1, was completed in October 1968, with the opening of a 56km (35-mile) section at its northern end between Rotherham and Leeds. The M6 was nearing completion with the Penrith bypass in Cumbria and the Walsall–Stafford link, and the M4 had by 1968 been extended into Wales with the opening, two years earlier, of the Severn Bridge.

In October 1968, London's Euston Station reopened after 'modernisation'. An iconic structure in the history of the railways, the terminus dated from 1837 when the London and Birmingham Railway was built. Euston was the work of William Cubitt, with a Greek-style Doric propylaeum, or monumental entrance, designed by Philip Hardwick and commonly known as the 'Euston Arch'. This formed a grand entrance to the Great Hall, with its double flight of stairs and allegorical statues gazing down on hurrying passengers. The decision to demolish Hardwick's mighty arch as part of Euston's makeover had enraged the architectural heritage lobby and saddened many passengers. The Grand Hall's replacement was a feeble and soulless concourse, while the 'public art' installed at the front of the station failed to inspire much affection. Critics of the Euston 'vandalism' included the poet Sir John Betjeman, and the outcry helped to stimulate campaigns by bodies such as the Victorian Society for a more sensitive approach to the marrying of old and new in public spaces.

While the train suffered a crisis of confidence, the car rode the crest of a wave. The car represented freedom; freedom to take the family away to the coast on holiday, or for a day trip to one of the growing number of 'attractions', whose owners had appreciated the potential for tourism in opening up homes and gardens. The 'theme park' was a concept in embryo. The Duke of Bedford had opened Woburn Abbey to the public in 1965, and now planned a new attraction – a safari park. Duly opened in 1970, it rivalled the lure of the lions of Longleat, the Wiltshire animal park opened by the Marquess of Bath in 1966.

A good day/night out

Social historians had by 1968 started to take 'pop culture' seriously. They surveyed and analysed the moneyed scene in London's smarter districts (such as Chelsea, rapidly acquiring an international reputation for coolness, not just artiness), where the glitterati glided in and out of fashionable boutiques, and discotheques (a word gaining currency since its arrival in English at the start of the decade). In most provincial towns and cities, and in the suburbs, 'going out' meant not a club or disco, but the cinema or a dance hall that changed little since the 1950s, or earlier. By 1968, some might have dropped the white-jacketed dance band playing standard strict-tempo numbers in favour of 'rave nites' with cheap local bands and groups, even a DJ, doing his best to mimic the presenters on pirate radio or Radio 1. Dance halls and small venues gave one-night gigs to local bands hoping to emulate Andover's Troggs or Ilford's Small Faces and show that any town, anywhere, could produce a chart-topping group.

Students had their union bars and 'hops', which sometimes attracted groups on their way up. Some bands preferred the university scene as more in keeping with the pseudo-intellectual flavour of their songs and album sleeve notes. Colleges themselves had produced bands of note – such as the Spencer Davis Group, from Birmingham University.

Youthful energies were usually fuelled more by alcohol than drugs, though July 1968 saw a rally to legalise marijuana at Speakers' Corner in Hyde Park, London. Heroin, cocaine and hallucinogens such as LSD were much talked about, but less frequently tried than newspapers suggested. Sexual mores were in flux, as the contraceptive pill offered women more protection, choice and control. 'Clubbing' hardly existed, as few towns yet boasted a nightclub.

Radio gave the first airing to music that people enjoyed on their nights out. Pirate radio had been spearheaded by Radio Caroline, set up in 1964, which for a time broadcast pop music from two ships (*Caroline* and *Mi Amigo*) moored offshore. Its DJs, including Tony Blackburn, Ed Stewart, Simon Dee, Emperor Rosko and Dave Lee Travis, had grown popular with young listeners. The government tried to shut the station down, on the grounds that it was unlicensed and was using frequencies in breach of international regulations. In 1967 Radio Caroline had been officially banned (and BBC Radio 1 introduced to fill the gap), but the station had continued operating until March 1968, when the two radio ships were boarded and towed to the Netherlands. Many of the pirate DJs found work with the BBC or other broadcasters, though the Caroline name continued in broadcasting in various forms into the twenty-first century.

Twenty-four-hour pop from a pirate radio station had not yet finished off 'traditional' dance music, and some youngsters still attempted to learn the steps demonstrated by their parents. Those wanting to see how it should be done could watch *Come Dancing*, which had been screened by the BBC since 1953. The 'disco' was still relatively new. But most wanted to buy pop records, and spent their money on vinyl singles (45s) and EPs as well as LPs (albums). They made their choices from the latest hit records, heard and seen on TV's *Top of the Pops* (from 1964) or, on radio, offered by *Pick of the Pops* (on BBC from 1967) with Alan Freeman. The more adventurous, with more cash to spend, dreamed of going to London – to Chelsea for the shops: the new Chelsea Drugstore, Stop the Shop (with its grey/black décor and revolving mannequin-adorned platform), I Was Lord Kitchener's Valet, Chelsea Girl, Top Gear or Kleptomania. Then they might explore the Soho clubs to hear the latest sounds: the Marquee, the Flamingo (though it cost 30s entry fee), and the Bag O'Nails. The well-heeled could still be seen at Sibylla's in Swallow Street, which had opened with much fanfare in 1966 and whose patrons included the Beatles, Julie Christie, Michael Caine and a host of other celebrities. Its brilliance was short-lived, however, with closure in 1968 as the trendy moved on to newer venues. The Cavern in Liverpool, where, according to legend, Beatlemania had all begun, was still going, but had only five years left in its original form; it closed in 1973.

Clubs for night, fields by day; free festivals were beginning to offer opportunities of a different kind. The summer rock festival scene was still in its infancy, and events comparatively small. Some venues tried, but did not repeat the experiment: in June 1968 at Burton Constable near Hull, fans could hear The Move, Marmalade, Family, Spooky Tooth and Fairport Convention. It was a one-off. On 29 June, Pink Floyd played the first Hyde Park free concert, an event fondly remembered by disc jockey John Peel, who recalled listening to the music from a boat on the Serpentine. Presented, as stated on the programme, by the Ministry of Works, the afternoon's bands included Roy Harper, Jethro Tull and T. Rex. For Pink Floyd, 1968 brought a break-up, with Syd Barrett, lead singer, leaving and being replaced by David Gilmour. The

Beatles no longer gave live shows; they and the Rolling Stones were busy in the studio, though the Stones were facing a line-up change, with Brian Jones restless prior to quitting the band in 1969. Elvis had been away some time, six years in fact, but in December 1968 he returned to his rock 'n' roll roots with an NBC television special, hailed by fans as 'The King's comeback show'.

Jimi Hendrix drew fans to Woburn in July, where the warm-up sets came from Geno Washington and the Ram Jam Band, and T. Rex again. August was the busiest period for travelling bands and hitchhiking fans. The Magical Mystery Tour festival in London featured the Incredible String Band, Traffic, Pretty Things and Fairport Convention. The bank holiday weekend saw the first Isle of Wight festival, an all-nighter and costing just £1 5s (£1.25). It drew a crowd of between 10,000 and 15,000. Opened by Jimmy Savile (then at the height of his fame as a *Top of the Pops* presenter) and compèred by John Peel, the festival acts included Jefferson Airplane (top-billed), with sets from The Crazy World of Arthur Brown, Pretty Things, The Move and (again, working hard) T. Rex. The Isle of Wight Festival snowballed, or mushroomed, in the following year, when the crowd topped 150,000 to see Bob Dylan and The Who. In September, fans splashed through the mud at the Bluesology Festival near Droitwich, to wave their arms and enjoy more of the same: The Move, Fleetwood Mac, Chris Farlowe and the Thunderbirds, Cliff Bennett, John Mayall's Blues Breakers, and Joe Cocker and the Grease Band. The success of these events set others thinking. In 1970 the crowds were off to Somerset, for the first Glastonbury Festival.

On a cushion of air ...

Hovercraft, as 'air-cushion vehicles' were known in the 1960s, seemed to offer a bright, adaptable amphibious transport alternative, especially for ferry services. No costly deep-water port terminal required (as for a ship), no runways (as for a plane), just a slipway to allow the craft to transition from watercraft to land vehicle, riding on its cushion of air. Another triumph for 'DIY' British technology; or so it seemed, when the latest and largest passenger hovercraft began cross-Channel ferry services in 1968.

Ever since 1959, the press had been excited about the potential of 'hovercraft'. The idea had been conceived by engineer Christopher Cockerell in 1954, when wrestling with the problem of how to improve the efficiency of a water-borne hull by reducing friction. He produced the concept of 'sidewalls' fixed along the hull, with flexible 'curtains' at the end to trap air inside. Using a hairdryer, empty coffee tins and kitchen scales, Cockerell had tested the theory of an 'annular jet' of air, found it worked and been granted a patent in 1955. Progress was, as so often with innovations, slow as Cockerell took his ideas around Whitehall and leading manufacturers, but he finally got the backing of the National Research Development Corporation and Saunders-Roe. In May 1959 the public was suitably wowed by the arrival of the world's first full-size hovercraft, the SRN1. The novelty of a craft able to skim with ease over both water and dry land was appealing. There was much talk of hoverships of ocean-liner dimensions, giant 'near-aircraft' carrying cargo and 'hovertrains' speeding along special tracks – all riding on cushions of air.

Water was in fact the best option for most hovercraft, which proved tricky to steer in confined spaces. The SRN1 crossed the Channel in July 1959, and a Vickers VA-3 design initiated a regular Dee Estuary ferry service in 1962, linking Wallasey and Rhyl. In 1968, a small SRN6 hovercraft went exploring in South America, covering over 3,200km (2,000 miles), travelling along rivers and negotiating rapids impassable for most conventional boats. By 1968 there were recreational air-cushion vehicles, and even a two-seater model that could be assembled in schools. There was also military interest from the navy, which saw potential for hovercraft in mine-clearing, anti-submarine missions in shallow coastal waters, and some also predicted a useful role in air-sea rescue, as well as army use for amphibious assault and logistical supply in difficult terrain.

The year 1968 seemed to be the start of something big for the hovercraft, and for the British Hovercraft Corporation based at Cowes. Into Channel-crossing service roared the newest and biggest hovercraft so far, the Mountbatten-class SRN4. Its capacity was impressive: the initial version could carry more than 600 people, or 250 passengers and thirty cars. Named on 31 July by HRH Princess Margaret, the new craft began a Dover–Boulogne service the next day. There were plans to operate a second route, from Ramsgate to Calais, using at least four craft. *Princess Margaret* was to be followed by *Princess Anne*, *Sir Christopher* and *The Prince of Wales*.

All seemed set fair for a new era of fast cross-Channel services. At this stage, Eurotunnel was still a distant prospect, and with chilly relations between the British Government and France's President De Gaulle, any imminent development of the long-mooted Channel Tunnel project seemed unlikely. And the SRN4 was an impressive beast. Powered by four stern-mounted Rolls-Royce Marine Proteus gas turboprop engines, it could belt its 168 tons deadweight along at well over 60mph (96km/h) and (its makers were confident) cope with the worst seas to be expected. Passengers could relax inside the cabin area, as the craft sped past conventional shipping. There was usually a lot of spray, but that all added to the sense of speed and adventure, and the four giant propellers at full pelt did make a lot of noise. The passengers would not be able to stroll on deck or spend an hour with a book as the white cliffs of Dover receded; sadly, such traditional ferry pleasures would not be part of the new hovercraft experience. It would be aircraft-style speed, no time for dawdling and dreaming: the crossing would be over in half an hour. The record time was in fact twenty-two minutes, set by *Princess Anne*.

In 1968 the world seemed to be hovering on the edge of a transport breakthrough. And it was British, and we had a world lead. Exports shimmered with the inviting allure of a desert mirage. 'Hover' was a new buzzword, and manufacturers hastened to apply it whenever they could. Cleaners, mowers, even beds – they all hovered.

It was a bright beginning. But sadly, the promise of 1968 was not fulfilled. Hovercraft were never entirely practical or economic for overland use, except in remote areas. The craft's noise became a problem at a time when people were growing more concerned about noise pollution. Channel service hovercraft continued into the 1980s, operated first by Hoverlloyd and from 1981 by Hoverspeed. The Ramsgate–Calais route proved uneconomic and the Ramsgate terminal closed after an accident in 1985 at Dover, when *Princess Margaret* was blown against a breakwater in the harbour and four passengers were killed. By 2000 the last SRN4 in service was retired.

9

September

EXITS AND ENTRANCES

Just not cricket ...

South Africa had played Test cricket since 1889, but by the 1960s opposition to the white minority government's apartheid policy had become more strident. The South Africans had already been forced out of the 1968 Mexico City summer Olympics. That winter, the MCC was due to send an England team to tour South Africa.

The touring party selection became a matter of national concern, since England's squad included a player born in South Africa but who had left to escape the apartheid legislation that barred him from playing for the national team. He was Basil D'Oliveira, of Cape Coloured background and so – as 'non-white' – not eligible for the all-white South African team. On arrival in England, D'Oliveira had qualified to play for Worcestershire and his form with bat and ball earned him his first England cap in 1966. He had cemented his place in the team, as an all-rounder.

In 1968 the looming controversy seemed to affect D'Oliveira's play. His form was patchy during the summer season against the visiting Australians, and he was left out of the second Test against Australia in favour of an extra fast bowler. However, conditions at the Oval in late August suited D'Oliveira's medium-pace bowling, so England captain Colin Cowdrey requested that he stand by for the final Test match. When batsman Roger Prideaux withdrew on health grounds, D'Oliveira was in the team and under huge pressure, in a match England had to win to square the series. He rose to the occasion, scoring 158 to put England in a winning position. Despite rain delays, the team clinched victory, thanks to some inspired bowling from spinner Derek Underwood. D'Oliveira chipped in with a vital wicket, the match was won, and the Test series squared at 1–1.

South Africa still loomed. Negotiation over the D'Oliveira affair had involved not only the British ambassador in South Africa but former British Prime Minister Sir Alec Douglas-Home, who had met South Africa's Vorster in March 1968. These contacts evidently persuaded the South Africans that the British cricket authorities were unwilling to ostracise them completely, and that sporting contacts would be maintained. Their main hope was that D'Oliveira would not be picked to play, particularly after an unimpressive tour of the West Indies the previous winter. It has been suggested that during the 1968 Test series, D'Oliveira was asked if he would consider switching allegiance, to play for South Africa instead of England. There were also reportedly offers of a lucrative coaching appointment, which would mean his dropping out of the MCC tour, even suggestions that D'Oliveira might be bribed to declare himself unavailable, or be persuaded to withdraw in the best interests of the game.

The England party for South Africa was due to be announced soon after the fifth and final Test match in England. Would D'Oliveira be selected? Officially, the South African Government had grudgingly indicated that the player would be allowed to tour. Prime Minister Vorster himself was said to be firmly and privately opposed, hoping MCC would ease the problem by not choosing D'Oliveira at all. This the MCC obligingly did, only days after the player's big score at the Oval. Their apparently odd decision was explained by saying that the touring party needed an additional bowler, not an all-rounder. D'Oliveira's exclusion was based solely on cricketing criteria.

D'Oliveira's omission split the press; some supported the decision while agreeing it was a close call based on merit. Others, openly critical, accused the MCC of caving in to South African pressure, and of what would today be called institutional racism. Saving the tour seemed to have triumphed over making an anti-apartheid statement. A deeply rooted belief within the MCC held that South Africa had to be kept 'on the field of play', not pushed into an isolation that would foster extremism. The contrary view, and that of the anti-apartheid movement, was that sporting isolation could be a powerful weapon in bringing about change. Those calling for the tour to be abandoned included the Reverend David Sheppard, a former England captain, who would soon be a bishop. The Anti-Apartheid Movement called on the prime minister to intervene, while D'Oliveira kept his own counsel, cheered by letters of support. He agreed to go to South Africa for the *News of the World*, and report on the series.

The cricketing gods then intervened. Warwickshire bowler Tom Cartwright was forced to pull out of the tour with an injury and the MCC announced that Basil D'Oliveira would go in his place. Sports minister Denis Howell insisted there had been no pressure from Whitehall. Now the outcry came from South Africa, as Vorster accused the England selectors of making a choice based solely on political grounds. He declared his government would not accept a team thrust upon them, calling it the team of the Anti-Apartheid Movement. South African press reaction was more nuanced; many feared the country now faced total exclusion from international sport.

The MCC refused to back down; the South Africans remained adamant. On 24 September the tour was cancelled. The MCC tour party went to Pakistan instead, taking D'Oliveira with them. He continued playing Test cricket for four years and for Worcestershire until 1979–80. It has been rumoured that he concealed his true age when working to make a cricketing career in England. He may have been 38 at the time of his England debut, and almost 40 at the time of the 'D'Oliveira affair'. Both his son and grandson later played county cricket.

Change did come. In 1969, South Africa's cricket authorities announced the first steps towards racially integrated cricket. Following demonstrations during the 1969–70 South African Springboks rugby tour of Britain, the planned South African cricket tour that summer was cancelled. After 1971, South Africa was virtually cut off from international cricket, finally returning to Test matches in 1991 with the ending of apartheid.

One leaving, one arriving

There was not, on the surface, much in common between Fred Trueman and Margaret Thatcher. Yet September 1968 was a turning point for both. For Trueman, it marked the end of a brilliant bowling career, with occasional ups and downs, as he retired from first-class cricket; for Margaret Thatcher, it marked a further step up the political ladder, as she became opposition spokesperson (spokesman in those days) for transport in Edward Heath's Shadow Cabinet.

Fiery Fred retired from his beloved Yorkshire with the team enjoying a run of success, winning its sixth county championship inside a decade, and defeating the touring Australians – a win that gave the fast bowler particular pleasure. Born in 1931, Trueman had made his England Test debut in 1952 against India, reducing the Indians to 0–4 in a shattering opening spell of fast bowling, and finishing with 8–31. In 1965 he had played his last Test, having the previous year become the first bowler to pass 300 wickets in international matches.

Analysts loved Trueman's bowling action; batsmen feared him, as he raced towards them in a manner which, if not calculated to intimidate, made most batsmen quake: a straight, long run, face set in a scowl, black mane of hair flopping. Trueman had great strength; his strong back and legs were those of a miner, as his father had been. His on-field persona, belligerent one moment, grinning the next, carried over into his off-field behaviour, and early in his career captains and selectors regarded him as an awkward customer. This probably cost him places on overseas tours, of which he made four: to the West Indies twice, and Australia and New Zealand, also twice. His fast-bowling partnership with Lancashire's Brian Statham was one of the most effective in world cricket; by the end of the 1968 season both 'Fred' Trueman and 'George' Statham had retired, Brian Statham's last county match being the August bank holiday Roses match against Yorkshire.

Frederick Sewards Trueman left superb statistics for the record books: sixty-seven Test matches, 307 wickets; 603 first-class games in all, 2,304 wickets. After retiring Trueman, rarely lost for words, moved into the commentary box with the BBC's *Test Match Special* team, where his trenchant opinions and frequent admissions that what 'modern' players were up to on the pitch completely baffled him, won him new fans. Fast bowlers were a frequent target, for who could compare with F.S. Trueman, in his own opinion, 't' finest bloody fast bowler that ever drew breath'.

Margaret Thatcher may have used different language, but her own opinion of herself seldom wavered. She had taken a while to break into politics. Margaret Roberts' first attempt at election to the House of Commons, in 1950 aged 23, earned her some notice as the youngest woman candidate, but she failed to dislodge her Labour opponent in Dartford. After trying again and losing in 1951, Margaret Roberts married Denis Thatcher and had twins, before finally being elected as Conservative MP for Finchley in 1959. She had secured a junior ministerial post, at pensions and national insurance, before the Conservatives were sent into opposition in 1964.

Though by no means close to Edward Heath, whom she was later to challenge and defeat for the party leadership, Margaret Thatcher was showing sufficient application and talent to merit promotion as a shadow minister. In 1965 she had shadowed housing (suggesting council tenants should have the right to buy); in 1966 she moved to the Treasury team, and in 1967 to shadow fuel and power. In November 1968, Heath moved her again, this time to shadow transport. In this capacity she pressed the minister, Richard Marsh, to confirm that police with breathalysers would not hide round corners to trap motorists leaving pubs. She also had occasion to complain about the late running of commuter trains on the Southern Region, and the lack of investment in transport. This, she thought, was the fault of undemanding bosses of nationalised industries (including the railways) who were too mean, or scared, to speak up and ask for money. *Hansard* (29 November 1968) quoted her remark that 'it has always seemed to me that the person who hollers the loudest is likely to get the greatest capital allocation'.

In September she was invited to speak to the Conservative Political Centre, during that year's Party Conference held in Blackpool. She took as her topic, 'What's Wrong with Politics?', and in her address showed that she was already formulating ideas about personal responsibility and less government that would mark her later years as prime minister. The great mistake of recent years, the up-and-coming politician declared, was that the government tried to provide or legislate for almost everything. She also had a bee in her bonnet about what is now called data protection: worrying about the amount of information the government now held about individuals, through too much form-filling and the imminent transference of personal data to computers. Above all, she said, politics needed enthusiasm; it was not enough for a political party to have reluctant support, it had to have enthusiasm. Her audience marked her out as perhaps one to watch for the future.

Basil D'Oliveira died in 2011, and Margaret Thatcher in 2013.

10

October

LEAPS INTO THE UNKNOWN

Rhodesia flies a new flag

Ian Smith's father left Scotland for the Central African colony of Rhodesia in 1898, and there Ian was born in 1919. In 1939 the young Smith signed up to train as a pilot with the RAF; he had an active war, was shot down over the Mediterranean, and spent some weeks with Italian partisans. After the war, he bought a farm in Rhodesia then went into politics. In 1968 this stubborn and dogmatic man was leader of the African colony's white minority government, and a very sharp thorn in the side of a British Government anxious to extract itself from colonial matters.

Over the years, from the 1920s, Britain had attempted to construct a federation in central Africa that could encompass the territories of Southern Rhodesia (now Zimbabwe), Northern Rhodesia (now Zambia) and Nyasaland (now Malawi). In most other African ex-colonies, majority black nationalist government had taken power when Britain lowered its flag, but Southern Rhodesia was proving especially troublesome. The federation plan had not worked. Zambia and Malawi were both independent since 1964; only Southern Rhodesia remained a colony. The whites-only government wanted independence. Britain insisted that the wishes of the black majority must be respected in any post-colonial future. Talks got nowhere, and in 1965 Rhodesia's Ian Smith had made a unilateral declaration of independence (UDI) – an act condemned as illegal by London, which imposed trade sanctions, as did the United Nations.

Harold Wilson had met Ian Smith in 1966 on board a Royal Navy warship, HMS *Tiger*, but their meeting bore no fruit. Smith could see little he recognised in 1960s Britain, especially under a socialist government. Wilson had confidently predicted that the Smith regime would fall in weeks; he would not use force against the rebels, since sanctions would drain Rhodesia's economy, especially by cutting off oil, and its exports (which included tobacco) would be badly hit. These forecasts proved woefully inaccurate. Rhodesia's whites-only regime had an ally in neighbouring South Africa, and sanctions busting became almost too easy. In Britain, Smith had considerable support among some newspapers, which contrasted Rhodesia's prosperity with the 'chaos' in other African states such as the Congo.

Wilson set out in October 1968 to try again after two years with little contact with Smith. Wilson's insistence on NIBMAR ('No Independence Before [African] Majority Rule) had united many Smith supporters in Rhodesia. The October talks then came as something of a surprise, and Smith and his colleagues were flown in an RAF Britannia aircraft to Gibraltar, where the prime minister awaited them on HMS *Fearless*.

Wilson seemed to take a more emollient line this time, while sticking to the 'six principles' previously set out. In their earlier warship negotiations, the usually calm Wilson had grown visibly angry, feeling he was being made to look impotent by a tiny country's even tinier minority leadership, while the rest of the Commonwealth demanded Britain take decisive action.

Once again negotiations broke down. The Rhodesians were adamant that they could tolerate no 'outside interference', not even from the Privy Council in London, over matters affecting their constitution – which in effect meant how the minority government treated the non-white majority. Britain insisted that there must be safeguards for black Rhodesians, in and out of the Rhodesian parliament.

The talks ended with the hope that further negotiations would be held, perhaps in Rhodesia, though a wide gulf remained. The fresh talks never happened. On 11 November 1968, the third anniversary of UDI, Rhodesia adopted a new flag, replacing its 'Sky Blue Ensign', which still bore a Union flag in one quarter, with a new green-and-white flag bearing the Rhodesian coat of arms. The die was cast. There would be no settlement.

In June 1969, white voters said 'yes' to the new constitution, and in March 1970 Ian Smith declared Rhodesia a republic. A guerrilla war, simmering since 1965, flared more disturbingly in 1972, though Smith went on saying he did not believe majority rule would ever happen, 'not in a thousand years'. But in 1978, the Smith regime did a deal with black leaders to form a power-sharing government, but fighting continued until a peace agreement in 1979, and elections in 1980 that returned Robert Mugabe as prime minister-elect. Britain, now led by Margaret Thatcher, recognised the country's independence under its new name, Zimbabwe. Smith continued to be a thorn, this time in the side of the new government, until his death in 2007 at the age of 88. Robert Mugabe proved even more tenacious, holding on to power into the second decade of the twenty-first century, when well into his nineties.

Jackie seeks solace in the Aegean

On 20 October 1968, Jacqueline Kennedy married Aristotle Onassis. It was a very private affair, on the groom's private island in the Aegean Sea. On Skorpios, the family retreat of the Greek shipping tycoon, the bride could feel sure there were no cameras prying from behind bushes, no paparazzi waiting to pounce, no intrusive reporters asking questions. About forty guests attended the ceremony, performed by a Greek Orthodox priest, and among those watching were the bride's children, Caroline Kennedy and John Kennedy Jr.

The world wondered. Why had one of the most famous women on Earth, widow of the assassinated US President Kennedy, decided to remarry? And why this ageing Greek? Why Onassis? He was rich certainly, a millionaire who in the years since his birth in Smyrna in 1906 had made fortunes from tobacco and shipping, and was by the 1960s one of the world's better-known tycoons. He had been married before, but that marriage had foundered after his very public affair with the tempestuous opera star Maria Callas.

So how had Onassis, for all his reputed charm and kind nature, come to win the world's most celebrated widow? This was the woman who, as the wife of JFK, had been one of the youngest, most glamorous and popular First Ladies ever to redecorate the White House.

Born in 1929, Jacqueline Lee Bouvier, 'Jackie' as she was almost universally known by the 1960s, had enjoyed a privileged upbringing, and as a young woman in Washington had worked as a photo-journalist for the *Washington Herald-Times*, quizzing people about where they shopped, which hairdresser they used and what they liked doing when not shopping. She had gone to London in 1953 to cover the coronation of Queen Elizabeth II, and that year she had married an up-and-coming Congressman about to become Senator, John Fitzgerald Kennedy, the ambitious son of a ferociously political family. Marriage to John Kennedy had pitchforked her into the public eye, into a world of campaign speeches, caucuses, conventions, and finally her husband's inauguration into the presidency. While pregnancy had restricted her participation in the 1960 campaign, she had still been 'the campaign wife', the title used for her weekly newspaper column.

First Lady at only 31 with two young children, Jackie Kennedy turned the White House into a family home, but also enlisted historians and art experts to help restore and preserve the building. She had been turned into a fashion icon, hers one of the most recognisable faces in newspapers and magazines across the globe. She was intelligent, a conversational linguist, an apparently relaxed hostess and a huge asset to the president, at home and abroad. Golden couples, though, do not always enjoy lasting private happiness; the president's philandering had to be borne with a discreet resignation, yet they remained close.

In August 1963, Mrs Kennedy has suffered the tragic loss of their third child, a son born five and a half weeks prematurely, and who died within two days. After the death of her baby, the president's wife was offered help for her depression by an old friend: Aristotle Onassis. He invited her to recuperate on his yacht and she accepted, with her husband's approval, though in the face of some public and government criticism. She returned to the United States on 17 October 1963, and a month later was at JFK's side for his politically important visit to Texas. On 22 November, the president was assassinated.

The death of the president turned the First Lady into a tragic heroine; photos of her in Dallas, in the presidential car, cradling her mortally wounded husband as the motorcade swept on, then, in the hours that followed, of her with the new president, and again at the funeral, were front-paged everywhere and etched into people's memories. She had become the face of the tragedy. Later, in an interview, it was she who referred to the couple's time in the White House as 'Camelot' – the president was said to have been fond of the Broadway musical about King Arthur and Guinevere.

Her position in the new Johnson era was never going to be easy. The new president offered her diplomatic roles as ambassador to France or Britain, but she declined, busying herself with the Kennedy legacy and raising her children. She was close to her brother-in-law, Robert Kennedy (the two sued the publishers of a book about the assassination, demanding changes in passages said to refer to JFK's private life), and his murder in June 1968 was a second, devastating blow. Her depression and misery were such that, according to reports, she had a morbid fear that the Kennedy children would inevitably become targets for killers.

And then she turned to Onassis. Rich and powerful, he could offer her privacy and security. But to some hostile critics it seemed like flight, even betrayal. The marriage was not well received on the whole by the US media. Onassis was divorced; she was a Catholic. In some quarters there was an unpleasant undercurrent of snobbery, even xenophobia. What was the former First Lady doing, marrying this foreign shipowner? She received less sympathy than perhaps she deserved. The Onassis lifestyle was also pored over critically, as they moved between homes in New York, New Jersey, Paris, Athens, Skorpios and the Onassis yacht *Christina O.*

Until 1980, Jackie maintained a close relationship with Edward (Ted) Kennedy, the surviving Kennedy brother and political hopeful, but the press gradually lost interest in her own comings and goings. Her marriage to Onassis lasted seven years, until his death aged 69 in 1975. She eventually returned to live in the United States until her own death, aged 64, in 1994.

Higher and higher at the Mexico Olympics

Before 1956, every Olympics had been staged either in a European city or in the United States. The 1956 Games had gone to Melbourne, Australia; the 1964 Games to Asia for the first time, to Tokyo. The 1968 host was to be Latin America. From the 1940s to the 1960s, Mexico City had enjoyed an economic boom and its selection seemed to provide an additional bonus.

Mexico City has several claims to fame: one of the mega-cities of modern times with a metropolitan area population of around 20 million; built on the site of the Aztec imperial capital of Tenochtitlan; but also one of the highest capital cities in the world, situated in a natural basin 2,240m (7,349ft) above sea level. The city's altitude is noticeable to any visitor more accustomed to lower-level living, and so is the air pollution, intensified by the effect of the enclosing ring of mountains that trap industrial and vehicle emissions within the city's natural bowl. The city has long-standing social problems, including overcrowding, crime and traffic congestion.

The city might therefore have seemed an unlikely choice for the Olympics, but its selection as host for the 1968 Summer Games was a move by the International Olympic Committee to take the Games into new regions of the world. The 1968 Games were officially the Games of the 19th Olympiad since their revival in 1896 as four-yearly events. As the scheduled Olympics in 1916, 1940 and 1944 were never held (because of war), the Mexico Games were the 16th of the modern era and turned out to be among the most memorable.

The 1964 Tokyo Games had been free of any political controversy. Not so in 1968. Mexico's Games seemed to reflect international tension and domestic disquiet. The most visual demonstration came during the medal ceremony for the men's 200m. American sprinters ran in first and third in this final, and on the winners' podium, gold medallist Tommie Smith and bronze medallist John Carlos raise clenched fists in a Black Power salute during the playing of the US national anthem, to show solidarity with American civil rights activism and to protest racism in their home country. The US Olympic Committee, pressured by the International Olympic Committee, suspended both athletes, but the incident was indelibly associated with the 1968 Games, shown as it was on global television and front-paged across the world's newspapers.

It can be agreed that, ever since 1968, the Games have rarely ceased to be politically charged (as well as prohibitively expensive). The 1972 Games saw the Munich terrorist attacks on the Olympic Village; in 1976 at Montreal there was a boycott by African countries; in 1980, a US-led boycott of the Moscow Games and, in 1984, a retaliatory boycott by the USSR and others.

Before the 1968 Games, commentators in sports media had been concerned about the effects of high altitude on athletes from low-level altitudes competing in endurance events. On the track, distance runners used to living and training at altitude were much more at ease. Australian world record holder Ron Clarke, running himself into near fatal exhaustion in the 10,000m race, could not force his body to keep pace with the Kenyans and Ethiopians. Kenya's Kip Keino ran away with the 1,500m ahead of world record holder Jim Ryun (USA).

Altitude had a startling effect on the explosive field and sprint events. New world records came in the men's 200m (Tommie Smith, USA); men's 400m (Lee Evans, USA); 800m (Ralph Doubell, Australia); and 400m hurdles (David Hemery, GB). Hemery won gold in the men's 400m hurdles with a new world record of 48.1 seconds, a full second faster than the previous time. There were new world records, too, in the men's relays (4 x 100m and 4 x 400m). In the women's track and field, Wyomia Tyus (USA) broke the women's 100m record, and helped the US team do the same in the sprint relay; the 200m world record also fell, to Irena Szewińska of Poland. Britain's favourite for gold, Lillian Board, was narrowly beaten by Colette Besson of France in her 400m race, but the women's long jump record went too, with a leap of 6.82m (22ft 4½in) from

Viorica Viscopoleanu of Romania. But that seemed as nothing by comparison with the most astonishing leap of all across the Mexico City arena.

On 18 October, long jumper Bob Beamon (USA) leapt an incredible 8.90m (29ft 2½in) to win not only the gold medal, but instant fame. Before Beamon, no athlete had jumped further than 8.5m (28ft). Suddenly, in one bound, the American had catapulted the record a further 50cm (21in) into the 8.8m (29ft) zone. It was dispiriting for his rivals, aiming at their very best to put in leaps of '27 foot something' (8.3m plus). Now the mark was 8.8m and beyond, and Beamon's seemingly unbeatable record remained so in fact for twenty-three years. Records are made to be broken, but on that day in October 1968 it seemed to many long jumpers and fans alike that this one event at least had been practically killed off for the foreseeable future. Beamon's jump was so long that officials had to resort to an old-fashioned steel tape to measure it. It was, not surprisingly, the finest few seconds of Beamon's life. He was unlikely to repeat it, and didn't, retiring soon afterwards.

Beamon's stratospheric leap was the most eye-catching consequence of the so-called 'oxygen debt' effect on athletes performing at over 2.1km (7,000ft) above sea level. Runners in the distance races, such as Ron Clarke, were said by medical experts to suffer a 10 per cent decrease in oxygen intake; athletes used to living and training at altitude, such as the Kenyans, were less affected than those acclimatised to low-level living. The effect of the 'impact' events was especially dramatic, with records in the sprints and jumps – and of course, Beamon's extraordinary leap into the far distance.

Equally enthralling was the performance of a largely unknown US high jumper. He startled stadium crowds by approaching the bar in a curving run, then twisting and, with his back to the bar, heaving head and shoulders over first before 'flopping' his body over into the landing area. The previously accepted style had been the 'scissors', where the jumper took off facing sideways to the bar and in effect tried to step over it. Beginning his athletics career as a scissors-jumper, Dick Fosbury later experimented with a laid-back, shoulder-first approach. Using it, he broke the Olympic record, and the 'Fosbury Flop' became the standard style for all those attempting to defy gravity and jump a bar higher than their own head.

If Beamon was the star of Mexico City, then Jean-Claude Killy had been the sensation of the Grenoble Winter Games. With three gold medals, the

French skier became poster boy for the Alpine events, while the cognoscenti applauded the Italian bobsled winner, Eugenio Monti, who at the age of 40 won a first Olympic medal after nine world title successes. There was equal praise from a rapt TV audience for figure skater Peggy Fleming (USA) and the pairs medallists Oleg and Ludmila Protopopov (USSR), who retained their title at the comparatively advanced ages (for skaters) of 35 and 32.

No Olympics, not even snowy ones, were ever free of controversy, and it was often the East Germans who provided it. There was undisguised suspicion of East German methods, both in training and medication, in their efforts to demonstrate Communist superiority over the West. At the Winter Olympics, the row broke over the luge toboggan event. Melting snow had affected the course's condition, which helped no one, but then three East German women were disqualified for cheating – by heating the runners of their toboggans to make them go faster.

11

November

IF AT FIRST YOU DON'T SUCCEED ...

Nixon wins the US presidential election

Social media and reality TV stars may not have featured in 1968, but celebrities most certainly did. To be a celebrity in that year usually meant winning or losing something; being arrested; getting the sack or resigning; encouraging revolution or cracking down on it. Politicians on the whole were still wary of, and not very good at, television. British Prime Minister Harold Wilson was comfortable in front of the camera and an interviewer, even a hostile one. Opposition leader Edward Heath looked much less at ease.

Richard Nixon had suffered death by television in 1960, when challenging John F. Kennedy for the US presidency. That year saw the first television debates between rivals for the White House; Kennedy was the more photogenic and assured in the TV studio. Nixon, despite his experience as vice president to Eisenhower, came across as ill at ease, even shifty, looking sweaty and in a need of a new shaver.

By 1968 TV interviewing styles had moved on, and so had Nixon. He was back in the race for the White House again as the Republican nominee, having reinvented himself since his defeat by Kennedy – which had actually been one of the narrowest in US electoral history (Nixon winning twenty-six states against Kennedy's twenty-two, but losing on electoral college votes).

Returning to life as a New York City lawyer, Nixon had watched Barry Goldwater crushed by the Democrats and Lyndon Johnson in the 1964 presidential election. He emerged from the post-election bickering as the candidate most likely to draw together the disparate liberal and conservative wings of the Republican Party. In February 1968 Nixon announced his intention to run again, defying doubters who thought him a loser by coming through the primaries in impressive style. He shrugged off his challengers: Nelson Rockefeller from New York and Ronald Reagan from California – the former Hollywood actor making his first serious move towards national political leadership.

This time, it was Nixon who had the grin and the close shave. He went into the election as probably the most experienced politician ever to seek the presidency. Having been elected to Congress in 1946, as vice president

(1953–61) he had been a frequent visitor to foreign countries, friendly and hostile, including a journey to the USSR in 1959.

The 1968 election has been called one of the most chaotic in US history. Johnson should have been a shoo-in for the Democratic nomination, but the darkening situation in Vietnam and unrest on college campuses and in the cities undermined the Texan's will to stay on. When he withdrew from the race, it was thrown open to the unlikely radical Senator Eugene McCarthy, who announced he would seek the Democratic nomination. Soon McCarthy had the vocal support of hundreds of students – some of whom trimmed their long hair to present a clean-cut doorstep appearance as they went out on the stump to rally anti-war voters to the McCarthy banner. McCarthy's success in the New Hampshire primary in March, where he picked up 42 per cent of the votes, had been a kick in the teeth for the incumbent president. Others now entered the arena: Bobby Kennedy and, after Johnson's withdrawal, Vice President Hubert Humphrey.

Kennedy looked to be prime favourite. To the glamour of the Kennedy name, Bobby brought years of electioneering know-how, having been campaign manager for his brother in the 1960 presidential battle. He took two primaries, as did McCarthy, and then scored the big one – California. That put him within a whisker of securing the nomination. But then he was gunned down in a Los Angeles hotel.

Kennedy's death left Humphrey as the establishment Democrat choice. Humphrey had incurred liberal wrath for his support of Johnson's Vietnam strategy, but his record on domestic issues was solidly liberal. The climactic Democratic Convention in Chicago drew hundreds of protesters, mostly anti-war, determined to see the Democrats shift their position on Vietnam. The Chicago Police Department viewed the protesters with suspicion, and waded in with their nightsticks (truncheons). The beatings and arrests spilled over into the Convention itself – hardly the best of atmospheres in which to accept the nomination, but Humphrey went ahead anyway.

The 1968 election was Nixon's last throw, and he knew it. Surprising many, he chose a relative unknown as his running mate: Spiro T. Agnew, Governor of Maryland. It was not a good choice in the long run. Agnew survived a first term but in 1972 became the first vice president to resign, after being accused of graft and tax fraud.

On the other side, the Democrats had to reshuffle their cards following President Johnson's decision against seeking re-election. It was not exactly 'Buggins's turn' but it was hardly unexpected that Vice President Hubert Humphrey got the Democratic nomination. A liberal who had loyally stood by Johnson since 1964, Humphrey was not exactly a whipper-up of wild enthusiasm, but he was tried and trusted. The Democrats were not yet ready to go the whole hog and choose the 'peace candidate', Eugene McCarthy.

Both candidates in 1968 made peace in Vietnam their main election promise. Neither was altogether clear as to how peace would be achieved, but bringing the troops home was a popular message. Nothing else seemed to matter so much. Humphrey offered more progress on civil rights; Nixon spoke in vague terms of 'internationalism', and getting other nations to share America's (self-imposed) burden of maintaining world peace.

The November election finally ended Nixon's years as runner-up, stand-in, loser. He won. Not massively in terms of popular votes – only 511,000 votes separated the two – but clearly in electoral votes (301 to 191 for Humphrey). An independent candidate, George Wallace, picked up forty-six electoral votes, but Nixon was home and dry. At last he would walk into the White House hailed as the chief. He had set out an ambitious programme in foreign policy – first and foremost, ending the war in Vietnam, but also improving US relations with China and the USSR. His 'Vietnamisation' policy did not bring immediate results, and violent protests continued across America for the next two years as the war lurched towards its messy conclusion in 1973–75. But in 1968, all that lay ahead. For now, as Christmas approached, and an inauguration speech beckoned, President-elect Richard Nixon could reflect on a long road successfully travelled, and maybe a bright sunlit upland ahead. But along that road into the future was a warning sign. And it read: Watergate.

The Watergate Scandal, arising from a break-in at Democratic HQ in the Watergate complex in Washington DC (17 June 1972) would bring down Nixon and end his presidency with his resignation and disgrace in August 1974.

Two writers seeking a reputation

Towards the end of 1968, the deaths of two eminent writers were reported. Both authors were household names, having enjoyed commercial success worldwide, but critical acclaim had been less fulsome at times, and at their deaths their reputations were ripe for reassessment. One was the children's writer Enid Blyton, the other the Nobel Laureate, novelist John Steinbeck. Blyton died in November, Steinbeck in the following month. At 71, Blyton was by five years the senior of the two.

Steinbeck was a grand old man of American literature, bracketed with fellow Nobel Laureates Ernest Hemingway and William Faulkner as the great American novelists of their generation. Steinbeck's golden years were the 1930s and 1940s; his books had been filmed, staged in the theatre, immortalised by inclusion on school and college syllabuses. Many critics had long decided Steinbeck's best writing was a distant memory, but the obituaries were respectful nonetheless; books such as *Of Mice and Men* and *The Grapes of Wrath* had earned him a place of honour in the twentieth century's literary pantheon.

Views about Enid Blyton were more divided. No one could doubt her commercial worth; she had enjoyed early success, earning in 1930 over £1,000 a year from writing, at least three times the amount most writers could hope for. Her output was phenomenal, and few children's bookshelves were without a Blyton or two tucked away on them. Merchandising had boosted her success, through toys, television and film adaptations of her most popular creations, such as Noddy and the Famous Five.

And yet, there were reservations, even disdain, especially from the literary and educational establishment, who turned up their noses and sent Enid Blyton to the naughty step for political incorrectness. Critics discovered in her books evidence of racism, sexism, violence and stereotyping, and by the 1960s had decided that Blyton books were in the main quite out of step with the modern world. Her sales, however, continued.

Enid Blyton, daughter of a cutlery salesman, was born in 1897 in East Dulwich and grew up in Beckenham. After training as a teacher, she had begun to publish in the 1920s, contributing to magazines. Key markers along the road to success had been her years as editor of *Sunny Stories*, then books such as *The Enchanted Wood* (1939), *Five on a Treasure Island* (their debut 1942), *First term at Malory Towers* (1946) and (his first appearance) *Noddy Goes to Toyland* (1949). The last 'Five' book had been published in 1963; the final 'Noddy' (*Noddy and the Aeroplane*) in 1964. Enid Blyton died at a Hampstead nursing home on 28 November 1968.

Less than a month later, on 20 December, John Steinbeck's final page was also turned when the writer died in New York City. It was six years after he had been awarded the Nobel Prize for Literature (1962), on which occasion the *New York Times* had commented that the award was almost posthumous, Steinbeck's best work being two decades or so behind him. Laureates, especially in the world of literature, are rarely rewarded when at their peak of performance, and Steinbeck's award was regarded as a recognition of his work in the 1930s and 1940s. Then he had been hailed by most critics as a proletarian writer, the standard-bearer for 'people culture', charging the barricades of bourgeois literary elitism. His California was far removed from the glitz of Hollywood, then or now. It was a world of itinerant farm workers and ranch hands, the poor and often exploited 'bindlestiffs' who travelled the rural byways looking for jobs. His was the America of the Depression, captured in photo essays by Dorothea Lange and others. *Of Mice and Men* (1937) and *The Grapes of Wrath* (1940) made Steinbeck a celebrity, but in later years he presented a somewhat gloomy figure, not liking much about modern life, disappointed that American prosperity had simply replaced poverty with 'too many THINGS'. He had kept in the public eye – the film of *East of Eden* (1955) starred Hollywood's meteor James Dean – but Steinbeck had never seemed comfortable as a public figure, nor was he ready publicly to sign petitions against US involvement in Vietnam, explaining that he preferred not to sign anything he hadn't written himself.

Like Blyton, Steinbeck had, for different reasons, fallen foul of the establishment. Although *The Grapes of Wrath* had won a Pulitzer Prize, his portrayal of the hapless Joad family, exiled from their failed farm by drought, dust and unfeeling bankers, had attracted a hail of criticism from the US Senate and preachers alike, who saw its 'message' as one of subversion. The book was banned in some libraries as being 'Red' propaganda.

The tale of three queens

Time was when every visiting Hollywood star stepped off a liner at Southampton Docks into the crackle of flashbulbs; the glamour of a 1930s Atlantic crossing persisted even beyond the war years – albeit briefly. Even in the 1960s most people might still name the world's biggest ocean liners: *Queen Mary* and *Queen Elizabeth*, Cunard's two super-queens, British and proudly so.

The two great ships had queened it over the Atlantic route for three decades. With few rivals, their aura inspired a fan base which included millions who had never set foot upon their well-kept decks, danced in their ballrooms, or dined in style while the ship ploughed across the North Atlantic as fast as most cars could manage on an A road.

Cunard's *Queen Elizabeth*, weighing (or displacing) 83,000 gross tons, was until 1968 the largest passenger vessel in the world, and probably the most famous. When launched in 1936 she was slightly bulkier, though about 3m (10ft) shorter than her older sister-ship *Queen Mary*. Both Cunarders could in their prime claim to be the largest liners afloat. *France* (1961) was longer, but lighter; the *United States* (1952) was slightly faster, and in 1968 still the holder of the Blue Riband for the fastest crossing of the Atlantic (three days, ten hours and forty minutes).

Yet by 1968, the dream was over. One queen had already left the stage; her sister was about to steam into the sunset. *Elizabeth*'s reign as ocean queen had been brief. She succeeded *Queen Mary* as Cunard flagship in 1946, but her early years were overshadowed by the Second World War, and later years by economic uncertainty caused by falling passenger numbers as more and more travellers chose to cross the Atlantic by an eight-hour flight rather than a four-day sea voyage. With neither queen now seen as economic, Cunard took the decision to retire both ships, while pacifying critics by announcing a new liner built to combine Atlantic passenger services with the growing and more profitable holiday-cruising business.

Queen Mary was first to go, in 1967, sold off and translated from ocean greyhound (holder of the Blue Riband from 1938 to 1952) to dry-docked tourist attraction. Her new home was at Long Beach, California, her interior gutted and reconfigured to metamorphose the great liner into a hotel, museum and entertainment complex – officially 'a building' so far as union regulations went.

The fate of *Mary*'s even larger – and younger – sister seemed at first to be parallel. In November 1968 *Queen Elizabeth* made her final transatlantic run. Then she was sold to a syndicate of US businessmen whose dream was to move her to a Florida tourist resort as a moneymaker. When the dream soon faded, the ship became a forlorn, rusting hulk, until after two years a new buyer came along – Chinese tycoon Y Tung. His idea was to move *Queen Elizabeth* to Hong

Kong, to become a floating school under the name 'Seawise University'. The construction gangs moved in and then, in January 1972, disaster: fire broke out over the ship, virtually destroying it. Some scrap was salvaged, the rest left on the harbour bottom to be covered by subsequent development.

It was a sorry end to a story that had begun with such promise when *Queen Elizabeth*, the world's biggest vessel, was proudly launched in September 1938 down John Brown's Glasgow slipway. Her passenger-carrying voyage was scheduled for 1940, but war began in September 1939 while the great ship was still being fitted out. Her gleaming paintwork had to be covered over with battleship grey, and in the greatest secrecy – for fear of German attack – the new Cunard queen steamed direct from Scotland to New York. There in harbour, *Queen Elizabeth* was berthed alongside *Queen Mary* and the French liner *Normandie* – a unique gathering of the world's three largest ocean liners.

During the Second World War, both queens were used as troopships, their high speed (average 31 knots, roughly 35mph/56km/h) enabling them to outrun German submarines as they zigzagged across the Atlantic. Their carrying capacity was astonishing: on one wartime voyage, *Queen Mary* carried 16,000 US troops (equivalent to an entire division).

When *Queen Elizabeth* returned to peacetime duties in 1946, repainted in sparkling Cunard livery and with interior rooms and cabins restored to pre-war elegance, the ship enjoyed an all-too-brief spell as monarch of the sea. But in the 1940s aviation was all the rage. First came larger long-range propeller-driven airliners such as the Boeing Stratocruiser and Lockheed Constellation, flying the Atlantic on the New York–London run. Not even the mighty queens could compete when speed mattered more to passengers than how many four-course dinners at sea they could enjoy.

As one queen departed, so another entered. Cunard's new queen, built with at least half an eye on cruising, was launched in September 1967, some obscurity surrounding the name. The Queen called the ship 'Queen Elizabeth the Second' at the naming ceremony, and newspapers printed it as 'Queen Elizabeth II'. Cunard chose the form *Queen Elizabeth 2* as the ship's name plate. And it was as *QE2* that the ship became generally known.

QE2 left Clydebank for Greenwich on 19 November 1968, carrying its first royal passenger, Prince Charles. The ship began sea trials, but they did not go well, revealing engine problems that caused delays and a postponement of *QE2*'s maiden voyage until May 1969. Slightly smaller than her namesake at 293m (963ft) and less bulky at 70,000 tons gross, *QE2* was to prove a popular ship with cruise passengers for many years. She too went to war, in the Falklands in 1982.

QE2 sailed as Cunard's flagship until 2004, maintaining the company's tradition of regular Atlantic crossings each year, alongside her cruise programme. Retired in 2008, *QE2* is currently in Dubai, her long-term future still uncertain. In her place has come the giant new *Queen Elizabeth* (2010) to serve alongside Cunard's other floating hotels, *Queen Mary* and *Queen Victoria*.

12

December

WHERE EVERY PROSPECT PLEASES?

Concorde vs Concordski

Major airlines were on the cusp of a significant decision: should they opt for greater speed and high-price customers, or for greater seat capacity and a jumbo-load of budget fare payers? Or both? Ever since the first generation of jet airliners – of which the British de Havilland Comet had been the first, but Boeing's 707 the most successful commercially – manufacturers had weighed the competing advantages of speed versus size. The British, still fascinated by speed, had in 1961 backed a joint project with the French to build an Anglo-French supersonic airliner. The US had also begun the design of a supersonic transport (SST), but later cooled on the idea of speed in favour of size.

The Anglo-French agreement had by 1964 evolved to involve four companies: BAC and Aérospatiale (to build the airframe) and Rolls-Royce and SNECMA (to build the engines). The incoming Labour Government then announced its withdrawal from the project, only to reverse that decision two months later. For a while the aircraft existed as two prototypes under two names: Concorde 001, being assembled in France; Concord 002 at Filton, near Bristol. Finally, with the Filton prototype virtually ready for trials, Tony Wedgwood Benn, Wilson's technology minister, declared that the 'e' spelling had it (for excellence as well as entente, and various other concepts, including Europe). From now on, the aircraft's official name would be Concorde.

So all was ready, and the two prototypes were about to emerge. The French aircraft had begun taxi trials at Toulouse when in September the first British Concorde 002 was rolled out of its hangar at Filton. Close behind it was the first pre-production Concorde, 01, with the 'droop-snoot' tilting nose that would become one of the aircraft's distinctive features.

And then, with all eyes focused on Concorde, an upstart rival stole the show. On the last day of 1968, at Zhukovski in the Soviet Union, a very similar-looking aircraft thundered into the sky. The Russian Tupolev Tu-144 was the world's first supersonic passenger aircraft to fly, though on its maiden flight it stayed subsonic, not exceeding Mach 1 until the summer of 1969. It was claimed to be faster than Concorde, with a cruising speed of 1,550mph (2,480km/h).

Concorde 001 flew for the first time in March 1969, and 002 in April that year. Despite the 1968 Soviet spoiler, Concorde was the first SST in airline service, in 1976, while the Russian aircraft proved unreliable and was used only on an internal route within the Soviet Union for about a year in the late 1970s. There were reported crashes, and the Russian SST never flew international commercial routes; it was grounded after 1978. The USA, having cancelled Boeing's proposed SST, the B2707, had gone for jumbo capacity, and in September 1968 rolled out Boeing's new 747. This new aircraft could carry 400-plus passengers and, while slower than either Concorde or 'Concordski', would prove a far more economical proposition for airlines.

Concorde's seductive luxury speed package – London to New York in under three hours, at more than 1,300mph (2,080km/h) – won high approval ratings from passengers, but Concorde could carry fewer than 150 passengers a trip, and its load factors were insufficient to win the airline orders the project needed. Its prospects were further dimmed by hostile environmental moves, banning supersonic flights and 'sonic booms' over land. Supersonic airliners, it was claimed, would wake people up at night, frighten children, frighten farm animals and even damage buildings. These objections restricted Concorde to trans-ocean routes, essentially the Atlantic. Like so many British aircraft projects of the 1960s, Concorde promised so much but in the end became an elegant and unique sidebar in the post-war aviation story. In 2003 British Airways and Air France retired Concorde, and the era of supersonic passenger transport, surprisingly brief, came to an end.

'Step Inside Love'

So sang Cilla Black, to introduce her BBC1 show. By 1968 Cilla was rapidly transforming herself from 'girl Beatle', the most recognisably Liverpudlian female singer of the 1960s, into all-round good sort and national treasure. Not for her the kaftans and tresses of hippiedom. Cilla's TV image reassured watching mums, dads and grandparents that, in spite of everything, the 1960s hadn't really changed very much. Cilla, while 'with it' and still a pal of the Beatles, looked and sounded like the girl next door, or your best mate on the assembly line, or even your auntie.

It was comforting for the older generation when others, like John Lennon, were beginning to look and talk oddly. ('He used to look so smart,' said my grandmother, 'when he and the others had those nice suits with the collars.') John was now paired with Yoko, hoping to bring world peace by giving press conferences from a bed. So how reassuring it was to turn on the TV and see Cilla, so wholesome, so 'ordinary'. You couldn't imagine her taking any of that LSD, or whatever they called it.

For music fans, 1968 seemed an interregnal year, a time of transition between the dreamy, gentle daftness of the Summer of Love (1967) and Woodstock (1969). Hippiedom, psychedelia, magic mushrooms, 'smoke-filled rooms' given new meaning – the extremes of pop fantasy had not yet turned the supergoup scene into a technicolour parody of itself.

With their *Sgt. Pepper's Lonely Heart Club Band* album behind them, and the end in sight for live shows and tours, the Beatles worked more as individuals, though combining in the studio to produce their new album. Yet 'Hey Jude' gave them a massive hit, and though reviews varied, the 1968 *White Album* with its plain black and white cover also sold well, its two versions of 'Revolution' chiming with the political tensions of the day. The Stones received plaudits for their *Beggars Banquet* album and produced a hit with the enduring 'Jumpin' Jack Flash'. If pop fans were sorry to hear Eric Burdon was quitting the Animals, there remained The Kinks ('Waterloo Sunset'), Cream's third album (*Wheels of Fire*, featuring 'White Room'), Jimi Hendrix with 'All Along the Watchtower', and Manfred Mann singing Bob Dylan's 'The Mighty Quinn'.

The old guard put up some resistance, for up bobbed veteran jazzman Louis Armstrong with a gravelly rendition of the glutinously sloppy 'It's a Wonderful World'. It was a hit worldwide. Feet tapped to the clear tones of Mary Hopkin singing 'Those were the Days', while a future rugby anthem was belted forth by Tom Jones, pounding his way through 'Delilah'. Even Des O'Connor made the charts, with 'I Pretend'. There were novelty songs, such as 'Lily the Pink', by The Scaffold, the curiously offbeat 'Cinderella Rockefella', by Esther and Abi Ofarim, and a hit western movie theme – 'The Good, the Bad and the Ugly', by Hugo Montenegro.

Musical tastes were eclectic in 1968. There was Rod McKuen, said to be the world's highest-earning poet/singer. Tiny Tim (aka Larry Love the Singing Canary) sold 150,000 copies of his album in fifteen weeks. This long-haired veteran regaled the media with his lifestyle recipe for clean living, which included a ninety-minute shower every day and a diet of pumpkin and sunflower seeds, wheatgerm and honey. One of the outstanding albums of the year was Simon and Garfunkel's *Bridge Over Troubled Water*. Mainstream US music recovered its nerve after the earlier 'British invasion' of bands. In any case, British musicians, lured to form supergroups were now taking up semi-permanent US residency.

US hits of 1968 were a mix of soul-searching and singalong: Otis Redding's '(Sitting on) The Dock of the Bay', Bobby Goldsboro's 'Honey', and 'Young Girl' by Gary Puckett and The Union Gap. A smash US hit of the year was Marvin Gaye's version of 'I Heard it Through the Grapevine', recorded in 1967; its release in 1968 gave Marvin Gaye his first US Number 1. The Beach Boys' California sounds of surf, sand, souped-up cars – and a little sex – were still selling, and they too went for 'peace and love', launching a new tour with the celebrated Maharishi. The plan was for the yogi to give a lecture at each Beach Boys' concert. Sadly, word failed to get around (or perhaps it did); poor ticket sales led to the tour being cut short.

Wholesomeness was good, but in the 1960s a tricksy reputation and some on-stage bad behaviour did a band's image no harm. Jim Morrison of The Doors got arrested on stage in Connecticut, when the local law decided his lewd behaviour had overstepped the mark. Brian Jones was arrested on a drugs charge, and Johnny Cash was making records in jail. By contrast, seriously silly songs deserved the description 'bubblegum pop', and with them were some equally silly band names. US group John Fred and the Playboys had a hit with 'Judy in Disguise with Glasses', a spoof on the Beatles' 'Lucy in the Sky with Diamonds'; the song's success condemned the band to be classed thereafter as a novelty act. And who now wants to admit remembering 'Yummy, Yummy, Yummy' by Ohio Express, or even 'Simon Says' by The 1910 Fruitgum Company? The Beatles could get away with it, letting Ringo take the lead on 'Yellow Submarine', originally recorded on their LP *Revolver* in 1966, and now back on the soundtrack for their animated film of the name, released in 1968. Intended mainly for children, it was at once subject to intense socio-political analysis.

To disabuse those who thought pop was getting soft, some seriously hard new bands arrived. One was a transformer, Led Zeppelin, which started in 1968 with ex-Yardbird Jimmy Page on guitar, Robert Plant (vocals), John Bonham (drums) and John Paul Jones (keyboards). Having begun as the New Yardbirds for contractual reasons, the band hit Scandinavia in September, began a first UK tour in October 1968, and then set off on their inaugural North American tour. For them the future beckoned, as it did for millions of others without rock glamour, hotel trashing or private jets. As ever, out with the old, in with the new.

So, what was new?

Every year brings a succession of entrances as well as the inevitable exits. At the time, some beginnings seem to mark real changes of direction, and prove to be so; others are merely side turnings, leading nowhere in particular, or dead ends, soon to be forgotten. December is a traditional time to look back, to reflect, and there was plenty to look back on as 1968 drew to a close.

Science was about to change lives, that was very clear. In 1968 a Wall Street brokerage company trialled a new security access system based on fingerprint identification – a first step towards what we now know as biometrics. The 1968 prototype was limited by 1960s computing power, but that too was changing fast. Pocket calculators were still novelties, and most commercial computers were the size of fridge-freezers. It took a roomful of such machines to calculate how to send astronauts to the Moon. So technicians raced to go small, and the new Apollo's spacecraft guidance computer (AGC) was the result of years of effort to miniaturise. It pioneered the latest integrated circuits and had core memory, and a two-digit input code system for the astronauts to type in as they communicated with the computer. Tiny for a 1960s computer, weighing only 31.7kg (70lb), the AGC was flight-tested during the year on the Apollo 7 and Apollo 8 missions, in preparation for the planned NASA Moon landing in 1969.

There were some computers small enough for home use, such as the Nova (32KB of memory) from Data General, and rumours emerging from IBM about something called a floppy disk. Even more significant was a report that scientists at American universities were designing a network, called Arpanet, to link computers in different locations. They wanted to message electronically; they were creating email, and the gateway to the world of Microsoft, Apple, and everything else in and out of Silicon Valley was beginning to open. In July, Gordon Moore and Robert Noyce set up Intel, the aim for their new corporation being to make new and better semi-conductors. The Intel memory chip made the corporation a world leader; in 1971 the company would produce the first microprocessor, a real revolution in computing.

On 9 December 1968, at a conference in San Francisco, Douglas Engelbart produced something else new – his idea for an 'online system' for video-conferencing. He demonstrated a gadget – a pointing device for use when working a computer, instead of using a keyboard; it was dubbed a 'mouse'. The conference also heard about 'hypertext', a kind of referencing system, the prototype for the hyperlinks familiar today, when people can navigate between searches using a mouse or a touch on the screen. All these concepts were a world away from life in the average office, where people had typewriters and telephones, and photocopying often required both a manual and considerable patience. But by 1968 it was clear change was on the way, even in Britain, where a young Alan Sugar started up his own business, calling it Amstrad, though at this stage he had not yet moved into personal computers. And still at school in Seattle was an American youngster named Bill Gates, getting his first hands-on computer time thanks to a deal his school had made with General Electric. Gates and friends quickly became hooked. They were soon so proficient that a local outfit hired them to check out its computers and look for weaknesses. Little did Seattle know where that boy was headed …

There were changes in medicine too, and these people could understand more easily. Epidurals were welcomed by women in labour. Organ transplants gave new hope to people with serious cardiac and other conditions: Christiaan Barnard had pioneered heart transplant surgery in South Africa the year before, and carried out his most successful procedure to date in 1968. Surgeons at the National Heart Hospital in London performed Britain's first transplant in May 1968. The patient died after forty-six days, and British surgeons proceeded cautiously over the next decade, though by the 1980s the procedure had become very much more successful. Surgeons at Cambridge performed Britain's first liver transplant in May – a further indication of dramatic progress in organ replacement.

In February, astronomers at Cambridge University announced that – only months before – they had discovered something new and strange in deep space. PhD student Jocelyn Bell and her supervisor Anthony Hewish had detected regular electromagnetic pulse signals from far-distant galaxies. The announcement was pounced on by overexcited media as possible proof of extraterrestial life – communication attempts perhaps. The astronomers explained: the sources, called pulsars, were rapidly spinning neutron stars; the pulses were mainly radio waves, but they were of natural origin. Their discovery confirmed a 50-year-old theory about the existence of these extremely dense objects, formed from the collapsed remnants of supernovas.

So no evidence as yet for aliens, but an eager market for speculation, in books such as *Chariots of the Gods*. In this 1968 bestseller, Erich von Däniken suggested all kinds of 'reasons' to prove that aliens from outer space had visited Earth long ago, and shaped ancient cultures and civilisations, from the Pyramids of Egypt to the Nazca lines of Peru. Scientists, including Carl Sagan, the American astronomer with his own plans for searching for extraterrestrials, wondered how people could be so credulous. Yet the book sold by the cartload, even though the author being jailed the same year for financial irregularities rather took the shine off his success.

Almost everyone can find something to be pleased about at the end of another year. 1968 was important for Laura Ashley, opening its first London shop. In September 1968 came a new listings magazine, *TV Times*. It was a challenger to the long-established *Radio Times*, which stuck with its original title even though TV now attracted far bigger audiences than radio. Even so, BBC Radio 1 celebrated its first birthday in September, with an audience of 27 million listeners. It was a good year for Alan Bennett, whose first play, *Forty Years On*, was staged in the West End with Sir John Gielgud and Paul Eddington, as well as the author himself.

Tom Stoppard, too, had a new play: *The Real Inspector Hound* starred Richard Briers and Ronnie Barker. Judi Dench sang on stage, as Sally Bowles in *Cabaret*. And Lionel Bart enjoyed a cinema triumph, with the success of the film version of his hit show *Oliver!*, first staged in London in 1960. The film, directed by Carol Reed, did full justice to Bart's original and, at his insistence, retained actor Ron Moody as Fagin, after Hollywood moguls had suggested replacing the 'unknown' Moody with a star such as Peter Sellers. The BBC's sixth season of *Doctor Who* began in August 1968, and running into 1969 saw Patrick Troughton complete his stint as the Doctor. Troughton had been the Doctor since October 1966, succeeding William Hartnell. Replacing him, eventually, as the 'Third Doctor', in January 1970, would be Jon Pertwee.

It was probably a disappointing year for those who thought things were going too fast, too far, and perceptibly downhill, when the new Theatre Act became law and the cast of the American 'tribal love-rock' musical *Hair* stripped off for the first time at London's Shaftesbury Theatre on 27 September. Veteran *Daily Telegraph* critic W. A. Darlington pronounced *Hair* 'a complete bore', but the 'strip-off' scene, where cast members appeared unclad from beneath a large sheet, gained enough publicity to draw the curious and kept the show running until 1973.

It's Christmas time

As Christmas 1968 approached, there was plenty to anticipate for television viewers young and old. There were the well-established favourites: *Animal Magic* on the BBC featuring avuncular Jonny Morris and artist-naturalist Keith Shackleton, *The Magic Roundabout*, *Tomorrow's World* (with Raymond Baxter and James Burke) and some now almost-forgotten soaps. One of these, *The Newcomers*, dealt with what was seen as a typically 1960s theme – relocation from city to country. It followed the fortunes of a manufacturing company that moved to rural Suffolk, with workers and their families following. The twice-weekly series featured a large cast including Judy Geeson, Wendy Richard, Glyn Edwards, Mark Eden and a young Jenny Agutter, who appeared during her school holidays. The young actress also won a part in the big-budget musical *Star!*, in which Julie Andrews played Gertrude Lawrence, and went on to secure the part of 'Bobbie' (Roberta) in a BBC TV adaptation of *The Railway Children*, a role she repeated in the 1970 film.

Christmas Day 1968 on BBC1 featured at midday *The Charlie Drake Show*, then *Top of the Pops '68*, with an all-star line up: the Beatles, Georgie Fame, Engelbert Humperdinck, Manfred Mann, Esther and Abi Ofarim, Cliff Richard, The Rolling Stones and The Union Gap.

The Black and White Minstrel Christmas Show took to the screen around lunchtime (2.10 p.m.); today this show is regarded with both disfavour and disbelief, because of the traditional black make-up worn by the (male) cast; the women dancers were the all-white Television Toppers. The Minstrels had been a hit on TV and records for years with their seamless reinterpretation of standards; it all seemed fairly harmless at the time, though in 1968 few younger people would readily admit to watching.

Following the Queen at 3.05, and how young she looked at 42 in only the sixteenth year of her reign, came a circus (Billy Smart's). The show featured not just trick riders, acrobats, clowns and an 'animal revue' with 'fox and goose, cat and dog, parrots and pigeons', but a fifteen-elephant pyramid! Val Doonican hosted *Disney Time* for children around teatime. Doonican was Ireland's answer to Andy Williams, known for his sweaters and for relaxing in a rocking chair while he warbled. There followed the pantomime *Humpty Dumpty*, starring, among others, Leslie Crowther, Lynda Baron and Reg Varney.

After a brief news, Judi Dench made an appeal on behalf of Christian Aid and then everyone settled down to enjoy *Christmas Night with the Stars* – who this year included Petula Clark, Derek Nimmo and Morecambe and Wise (then as much part of the festive foundations as they remain today). Also ever present was Ken Dodd, whose *Doddy for Christmas* show followed with a collection of supporting acts, among them the Diddymen, Watney's Silver Band, drum majorettes from Barking, various dancers and Judith Chalmers.

ITV had filled its afternoon with two films, a Tarzan adventure and *Lassie*, and it too showed a circus, before treating its audience to familiar fare: *Opportunity Knocks* and *Coronation Street*. It was then back to another film, a western, ending the evening with the Fay Weldon drama *Hippy Hippy Who Cares*, starring Julia Foster.

Back on BBC1, those still awake could rouse themselves to chuckle at Jack Lemmon and Tony Curtis (and Marilyn Monroe) in *Some Like it Hot* before the Christmas Day News, read by Robert Langley, and a Boxing Day forecast from BBC weatherman Bert Foord. The BBC's day was rounded off by *Quiz of the Year*, in which Ned Sherrin tested the wits and memories of two teams, including Richard Ingrams, John Wells and Willie Rushton, Mary Kenny, Linda Blandford and Neil Shand.

A feature of Christmas broadcasting across the channels was was 'Apollo Report' – updates on the NASA Apollo 8 mission to the Moon, then gripping the world's attention. This was real star-gazing.

Fly me to the Moon

It had been seven years since President Kennedy told the world America was going to fly men to the Moon, and would do so before the 1960s were over. At the time Kennedy made this bold promise, the United States lagged behind the USSR in the space race and to the president's critics it seemed rash, foolhardy – and, even if it came off, absurdly expensive. Anyway, what was the point?

The USSR had heavy-lift rocketry originally developed to launch long-range nuclear missiles. It had jumped into space in 1957 by launching the first satellite or 'Sputnik', and soon afterwards the first space-dog (Laika), while in 1959 it sent the first robot probe (Luna 2) to crash into the Moon. A second Soviet probe (Luna 3) then flew right around the Moon to photograph its far side, never before seen, since the Moon always keeps the same side facing Earth as it orbits our planet. When in 1961 Yuri Gagarin had become the world's first astronaut in orbit, Americans felt angry, shocked and nervous about the future. The public demanded action and so the president issued his call to the nation's space scientists. No expense spared, no effort shirked: the US space programme, initially divided between scientists and military, was to be accelerated ambitiously. By 1968 the Americans were definitely back in the race.

NASA had put Mercury astronaut John Glenn into orbit in 1962, and sent three other Mercury spacecraft into space by 1963. The Mercury was, however, a midget craft, barely big enough for one person. By October 1964 the Russians had shown their muscle, with their three-man spacecraft Voskhod 1, and in March 1965 achieved another first – when cosmonaut Aleksei Leonov stepped outside his orbiting Voskhod 2 craft to make the first spacewalk.

So far, the Russians had succeeded in snatching all the headlines: first satellite; first man in space; first woman in space (Valentina Tereshkova) in 1963. Most non-experts assumed that the Russians' next ploy would be a Moon mission. A landing by a robot probe (Luna 9) in 1966 seemed to confirm 'Red Moon' intentions.

To pick out potential lunar landing sites, it was essential to fly robot orbiters around the Moon, to survey the surface. The Soviet space team were set on the same course. But were the Russians intending to send unmanned probes to the Moon – or would they send cosmonauts to plant the red flag and demonstrate to the world the superiority of socialism?

NASA's Moon mission, so confidently promised by Kennedy, was given the name Apollo. Before a Moon craft could fly, however, a preparatory test flight series of a two-man craft, Gemini, was made from 1965 to 1966. These orbital flights provided astronauts with vital experience of duration (up to eight days) in space, and the crucial technique of 'docking' one craft together with another.

There are several theoretical ways to fly a craft from Earth to Moon: NASA selected the 'lunar-orbit rendezvous'. A giant (but as yet untried) Saturn 5 rocket would blast the Apollo craft on a course towards the Moon. Three astronauts would travel in a cone-shaped command module. Inside the bigger service module would be their vital supplies: oxygen, water, power and propulsion systems. The third and flimsiest section of Apollo, the two-man lunar module, was designed to be used only for descent onto the Moon's surface and (hopefully) a return ascent to rejoin the third astronaut in the 'mothership' module, orbiting above the Moon. An engine burn would then send the craft back towards Earth. Only the conical and heat-shielded command module could withstand the fiery re-entry into Earth's atmosphere, culminating in splashdown in the ocean.

It seemed far more complex to lay people compared to science fiction. Comic-strip heroes like Dan Dare simply walked to a rocket ship standing entire and erect at a futuristic space base, before soaring straight up, away from the Earth and out into space. In science fiction there was none of the humdrum reality of 1960s space technology, with multi-stage boosters on top of which perched an assemblage of modules. It seemed positively hazardous to have to detach modules at various stages of the flight. And the re-entry 'splashdown' in the sea, by parachute, could be anti-climactic.

The chosen strategy was complicated, especially so given the limitations of 1960s computing power, but NASA felt it had the crucial advantage of fuel economy, by landing only the smallest and lightest section of Apollo on the Moon's surface. NASA's confidence was dealt a near-fatal blow, however, on 27 January 1967 when, during preparations for the first full-scale Apollo test flight, a flash fire inside the still-grounded craft killed all three astronauts inside.

Their schedule in tatters, NASA engineers worked frantically to identify and fix the design fault that caused the fire, thought to be an electrical short circuit. A redesigned Apollo was test-flown unmanned. The Russians meanwhile suffered their own space tragedy, when only months after the Apollo fire, their Soyuz 1 spacecraft got into difficulties in Earth orbit. Attempting to land, the craft's re-entry parachute failed to open and the capsule crashed; cosmonaut Vladimir Komarov was killed. The Russians too had to rethink.

Even so, as 1968 began, the Americans were sure the Russians would attempt a 'fly-by' of the Moon, if not a landing. They redoubled their efforts. Having tested the redesigned Apollo in Earth orbit, they decided to go for broke, and commit the next manned launch to the Moon, not to land, but to fly around it. This was the task assigned to the Apollo 8 crew: James Lovell, Frank Borman and William Anders. Borman and Lovell had flown in space before, in Gemini 7. For Anders it was his first flight.

The lift-off of Apollo 8 on 21 December 1968 was watched by hundreds of thousands of anxious spectators around the Kennedy Space Center in Florida, and many millions around the world on television. Spaceflight was more than front-page news: it captivated television audiences with the drama of the rockets taking off into blue sunlit skies, the grainy pictures and crackling voices from space, the welter of facts and figures, the studio experts with their charts and explanations, the tension of re-entry, the relief at seeing a parachute descend, lowering a charred-looking space capsule into the waves. It was high adventure, enhanced by the 'right stuff' images of the astronauts, most of whom were ex-test pilots.

Whereas Soviet spaceflights were shrouded in secrecy, often revealed publicly only after success was assured, the Americans conducted their space programme in the spotlight of media interest. Success and failure were exposed to the full glare of publicity. Failure now would be even more costly, with three lives consigned to the unreachable void of space. Little wonder that Christmas that so many eyes turned to the heavens. For three days Apollo 8 journeyed towards the Moon, the first time a human craft had ventured beyond the protection of Earth's atmosphere. Every report, every photo, every engine burn, was followed with keen attention. Apollo 8 made lunar orbit safely, allowing humans for the first time to gaze down on the surface of a world not their own. As Earth came into view, rising above the rim of the harsh and barren lunarscape, millions on Earth gazed in wonder. Few had ever seen a photograph to match it for grandeur. And it was Christmas.

The astronauts broadcast home on Christmas Eve. The Moon they found forbidding – 'vast, lonely'. They took turns to read verses 1–10 of the Book of Genesis, on Creation.

Commander Frank Borman had been sick only hours before launch; no astronaut wants to start a space mission with nausea and diarrhoea. Luckily, a few hours' sleep had seemed to settle Borman's pre-launch ailment. With Moon orbit achieved, further nerve-racking moments were in store for those waiting at Mission Control and at home on Earth. Among the most nail-biting was when, out of sight of Earth, and out of radio contact, the Apollo 8 crew ignited the engine burn to blast them away from Moon orbit and send them home. When radio contact was restored, Lovell's voice reassured listeners: 'Please be informed there is a Santa Claus.' The burn had worked. Apollo 8 was on its way home.

Apollo 8's 'Earthrise' photo, taken by Anders, is one of the twentieth century's most iconic images. For the first time, humans saw their home in its entirety and appreciated its unique beauty. The photo was awe-inspiring not only in itself, but also because the viewer realised the risks involved in capturing it. The Apollo 8 crew had no 'lifeboat', no Moon-landing craft to move into should things go wrong. If NASA calculations were out, or the engine burn failed, Apollo 8 would have carried its doomed crew into infinity. There could be no hope of rescue. The risks were immense, but so were the rewards. Only twenty-four people have seen the Moon that close; Lovell, Bormann and Anders were the first.

Jim Lovell went on to command the near-disastrous 1970 Apollo 13 mission, which had to be aborted en route to the Moon after an explosion on board. That it got home safely was to the enormous credit of NASA engineers and the astronauts aboard.

Forty-five years later Lovell (then 85) said, 'The idea of bringing people together by a flight to the Moon where we encompassed everybody in our thoughts is still very valid today.' Of the mission's impact, Anders said, 'the most important thing is that we discovered the Earth.'

Less than six months after Apollo 8, and with two other Apollo flights proving that all the major components worked, Apollo 9 set out to fulfil President Kennedy's vow. On 9 July 1969, it took Neil Armstrong and Buzz Aldrin to the surface of the Moon. But it had been at Christmas 1968 that people's imaginations were captured by the sheer wonder of space, with those photos of Earth taken as Apollo 8 made its brave and lonely voyage out beyond the Earth and around the Moon. With all the conflicts and problems besetting the world, it made many pause, seeing the astonishing images of a green and blue planet floating in blackness, a speck of life within the immensity of a galaxy that science told them was just one of millions, even billions, in a universe of infinite possibilities. Enough to make anyone think, first-footing or partying that New Year's Eve, and looking up at the stars.

Appendix 1

A NEW WORD FOR IT

The year 1968 was rich in new words and phrases. A fortunate executive released from toil as part of a 'rationalisation' exercise might leave the desk with a 'golden handshake'. There might well then be a 'laugh-in' with friends at the pub; laugh-in could mean general hilarity, but for those who knew, it was also the title of a new US comedy show on TV: *Rowan and Martin's Laugh-in*. With money to burn, the departing executive could stop worrying whether lack of 'charisma' had prompted the sack, and maybe try to recapture lost youth by a spot of 'mind-blowing' dabbling in strange substances.

Also new in the 1968 lexicon were:

acid rock	pager
aerobics	pulsar
airbag	rip-off
cellulite	SALT (disarmament talks)
downplay	ufologist
gunship	wok
Hare Krishna	workaholic
kiss of life	yippie
maxi skirt	zap
morning-after pill	

Appendix 2

HIGHER AND HIGHER …

Ronan Point was at best middle-sized as tower blocks went, even back in 1968, at about 61m (200ft). Britain's highest building was the Post Office Tower (opened by Harold Wilson in 1965), a new London landmark which was 191m (626ft) high including its antenna. From 1966, up to 4,000 visitors a day went up to the top of the tower, to admire the view and the novelty of its revolving restaurant (which did not stay open beyond the 1980s). The tower itself remained London's tallest building until it was overtaken by the NatWest Tower in 1980. Since 2013, the Shard in London has been Britain's highest building at 310m (1,016ft).

In the late 1960s skyscrapers were still a novelty outside North America, where the majority of the world's tallest buildings were. In 1968 the world's tallest building was still the 1931-vintage Empire State Building in New York City, and it would continue to hold top spot for another two years, until 1970 – when the Twin Towers of the World Trade Center were completed.

Today, it is in the Middle East and Asia where cities compete most desperately to construct ever-taller pinnacles of concrete, glass, steel and plastic, to demonstrate human achievement – or vanity, depending on your point of view. In an age of ever-higher superstructures like the 2010 Burj Khalifa tower in the United Arab Emirates, at 828m (2,717ft), it's noteworthy that in 1968 the only structures in the record books that were higher than the Empire State Building were TV masts, and even the tallest communications mast in 1968 was almost 213m (700ft) shorter than the Burj Khalifa.

Appendix 3

BORN IN 1968

Among the newborns being cooed over in 1968 were those destined to become celebrities for one reason or another. Future stars in their cradles included the following:

Samira Ahmed	journalist
Gillian Anderson	actor
Mike Atherton	cricketer
Eric Bana	actor
Chris Boardman	cyclist
Rebekah Brooks	media executive
Darren Clarke	golfer
Brian Cox	scientist and TV presenter
Daniel Craig	actor
Victoria Derbyshire	broadcaster
Celine Dion	singer
Brendan Fraser	actor
Mel Gieldroyc	TV presenter
Mika Hakkinen	racing driver
Kate Humble	TV presenter
Nasser Hussain	cricketer

Hugh Jackman	actor
Ashley Judd	actor
Jason Leonard	rugby player
Adrian Lester	actor
Helen McCrory	actor
Kylie Minogue	singer
Al Murray	comedian
Marine Le Pen	politician
Sophie Raworth	TV presenter
Mary Lou Retton	gymnast
Guy Ritchie	film director
Julia Sawalha	actor
Will Smith	actor
Catherine Tate	entertainer
Matt Le Tissier	footballer
Kirsty Young	TV/radio presenter

Appendix 4

TWELVE THINGS YOU MAY NOT HAVE KNOWN ABOUT 1968 – OR HAVE FORGOTTEN …

Former 1950s rock star Tommy Steele appeared as a leprechaun in the 1968 musical *Finian's Rainbow*, starring Fred Astaire and Petula Clark.

During the summer of 1968 director Richard Attenborough and film crew were working in and around Brighton, filming *Oh What a Lovely War*, with much of the film shot on Brighton's West Pier (1866–1975) now collapsed.

John Hanson took the popular but hardly hip musical *The Desert Song* into the West End, had a hit, and followed it with *The Student Prince*.

The Who were in the studio from September recording their 'rock-opera' *Tommy*, released in 1969.

Red Alligator, ridden by jockey Brian Fletcher, won the 1968 Grand National at Aintree, having been third the previous year.

Lockheed's C5 Galaxy aircraft made its first flight. Hailed as the world's biggest military transport, the Galaxy set new records for cost overrun, and had a chequered service career.

Nigerian writer Wole Soyinka, later a Nobel Prize winner, was in prison in Nigeria, accused by the Federal Government of being a spy for the breakaway province of Biafra. He was released in 1969, after the Nigerian Civil War ended.

The longest track event for women in the 1968 Olympic Games was the 800m. No 1,500m race (introduced in 1972) and no marathon (not an Olympic event until 1984).

HMS *Scylla*, launched in 1968, was the last ship to be built in a Royal Dockyard, at Devonport. After being decommissioned, the frigate was sunk in 2004 off the Cornish coast, to become an artificial reef.

Britain's first sextuplets were born, in Birmingham in October 1968 – though three died soon after their premature birth.

A gallon of petrol (no litres then) cost 5s 5d – equivalent to 27 pence in today's money, though not in value. The average UK house price was less than £5,000 …

When Swaziland gained its independence in 1968, it was the last British colonial territory in Africa to do so, with the exception of Rhodesia (now Zimbabwe) which was still in the throes of its illegal UDI.

Appendix 5

SONGS OF THE YEAR: YOU MAY REMEMBER THESE FROM 1968, MONTH BY MONTH

January

'Fire Brigade' – by The Move
'Don't Stop the Carnival' – by The Alan Price Set
'Everlasting Love' – by Love Affair

February

'Rosie' – by Don Partridge
'Jennifer Juniper' – by Donovan
'Delilah' – by Tom Jones

March

'Step Inside Love' – by Cilla Black
'Green Tambourine' – by The Lemon Pipers
'Bend Me Shape Me' – by Amen Corner

April

'Jennifer Eccles' – by The Hollies
'Can't Take My Eyes Off You' – by Andy Williams
'A Man Without Love' – by Engelbert Humperdinck

May

'Blue Eyes' – by Don Partridge
'Little Green Apples' – by Roger Miller
'Captain of Your Ship' – by Reparata and the Delrons

June

'Mrs Robinson' – by Simon and Garfunkel
'My Name is Jack' – by Manfred Mann
'I Close My Eyes and Count to Ten' – by Dusty Springfield

July

'I'll Walk with God' – by The Bachelors
'Dream a Little Dream of Me' – by Anita Harris
'Hurdy Gurdy Man' – by Donovan

August

'I Say a Little Prayer' – by Aretha Franklin
'Hello, I Love You' – by The Doors
'This Guy's In Love with You' – by Herb Alpert

September

'It's in His Kiss' – by Betty Everett
'My Little Lady' – by The Tremeloes
'Dream a Little Dream of Me' – by Mama Cass

October

'A Day Without Love' – by Love Affair
'Les Bicyclettes de Belsize' – by Engelbert Humperdinck
'Red Balloon' – by The Dave Clark Five

November

'Build Me Up Buttercup' – by The Foundations
'I'm the Urban Spaceman' – by The Bonzo Dog Doo-Dah Band
'Ob-la-di-ob-la-da' – by Marmalade

December

'On Mother Kelly's Doorstep' – by Danny La Rue
'Something's Happening' – by Herman's Hermits
'Albatross' – by Fleetwood Mac

Appendix 6

AND THESE WERE THE BIG SELLING CHART-TOPPERS

UK Number Ones 1968

Artist	Title	Date	Wks at No. 1
Love Affair	'Everlasting Love'	21 Jan	2
Georgie Fame	'The Ballad of Bonnie and Clyde'	24 Jan	1
Manfred Mann	'Mighty Quinn'	14 Feb	2
Esther and Abi Ofarim	'Cinderella Rockefella'	28 Feb	3
Dave Dee, Dozy, Beaky, Mick and Tich	'The Legend of Xanadu'	20 Mar	1
The Beatles	'Lady Madonna'	27 Mar	2
Cliff Richard	'Congratulations'	10 Apr	2

Louis Armstrong	'What a Wonderful World'	24 Apr	4
Gary Puckett and The Union Gap	'Young Girl'	22 May	4
The Rolling Stones	'Jumpin' Jack Flash'	19 Jun	2
The Equals	'Baby, Come Back'	3 Jul	3
Des O'Connor	'I Pretend'	24 Jul	1
Tommy James and The Shondells	'Mony Mony'	31 Jul	2
Crazy World of Arthur Brown	'Fire'	14 Aug	1
Tommy James and The Shondells	'Mony Mony'	21 Aug	1
The Beach Boys	'Do It Again'	28 Aug	1
Bee Gees	'I've Gotta Get a Message to You'	4 Sept	1
The Beatles	'Hey Jude'	11 Sept	2
Mary Hopkin	'Those Were The Days'	25 Sept	6
Joe Cocker	'With a Little Help from My Friends'	6 Nov	1
Hugo Montenegro	'The Good, the Bad and the Ugly'	13 Nov	4
The Scaffold	'Lily the Pink'	11 Dec	3

Appendix 7

MOST-WATCHED TV SHOWS (DECEMBER 1968)

1.	*Coronation Street*	ITV	7.6 m
2.	*Coronation Street*	ITV	7.1 m
3.	*Father, Dear Father*	ITV	7.0 m
4.	*Sherlock Holmes*	BBC	6.9 m
5.	*The Val Doonican Show*	BBC	6.9 m
6.	*Till Death Us Do Part*	BBC	6.7 m
7.	*The Jimmy Tarbuck Show*	ITV	6.7 m
8.	*The Forsyte Saga*	BBC	6.6 m
9.	*Mike and Bernie's Show*	ITV	6.6 m
10.	*Frost on Sunday*	ITV	6.6 m

Sources: www.teletronic. co.uk /www.televisionheaven.co.uk

Appendix 8

UNIVERSITY LIFE

The number of universities in Britain doubled during the 1960s, to forty-six. All but two of the twenty-four new universities were founded before 1968 – institutions such as Sussex (1961), Warwick (1965) and Stirling (1967). Fewer than 9 per cent of the population were in higher education, with around 50,000 new graduates a year at the end of the 1960s (compared with around 17,000 in 1950, and over 300,000 in 2010).[1] New in 1968 was the New University of Ulster; and in 1969 the Open University came into being, very much the brainchild of Labour education minister Jennie Lee and Prime Minister Harold Wilson, enrolling its first students in 1971.

In 1968, university students were a fairly small minority, and generally regarded as privileged and as groundbreakers – many undergraduates being the first in their families to experience higher education.

---

1. Source: ONS/CSO Higher Education Statistics Agency
   Education: House of Commons Library: Historical statistics Standard Note: SN/SG/4252 2012.

Appendix 9

THE FOOTBALL LEAGUE DIVISION ONE 1968

Team	Played	Won	Drawn	Lost	Points
Manchester City	42	28	6	10	58
Manchester United	42	24	8	10	56
Liverpool	42	22	11	9	55
Leeds United	42	22	9	11	53
Everton	42	23	6	13	52
Chelsea	42	18	12	12	48
Tottenham Hotspur	42	19	9	14	47
West Bromwich Albion	42	17	12	13	46
Arsenal	42	17	10	15	44
Newcastle United	42	13	15	14	41
Nottingham Forest	42	14	11	17	41
West Ham United	42	14	10	18	38
Leicester City	42	13	12	17	38
Burnley	42	14	10	18	38
Sunderland	42	13	11	18	37
Southampton	42	13	11	18	37
Wolves	42	14	18	20	36
Stoke City	42	14	7	21	35

Sheffield Wednesday	42	11	12	19	34
Coventry City	42	9	15	18	33
Sheffield United	42	11	10	21	32 R
Fulham	42	10	7	25	27 R

R = relegated to Division Two

Division Two champions were Ipswich, also promoted were Queen's Park Rangers. Relegated to Division Three were Rotherham and Plymouth Argyle.

Division Three champions were Oxford United, also promoted were Bury.
Relegated to Division Four were Grimsby, Colchester, Scunthorpe and
Peterborough (who had been docked 19 points).

Promoted from Division Four: Luton Town, Barnsley, Hartlepool United and Crew
Alexandra.
Bradford Park Avenue finished bottom, but no club was voted out of the Football
League that year.

In Scotland, Celtic finished champions (played 34, won 30, drawn 3, lost 1), with
63 points, two points ahead of Rangers (won 28, drawn 5, lost 1).

Appendix 10

THE WILSON CABINET 1968

Prime Minister and First Lord of the Treasury	Harold Wilson
Secretary of State for Foreign Affairs	George Brown/Michael Stewart
First Secretary of State	Michael Stewart/Barbara Castle
Chancellor of the Exchequer	Roy Jenkins
Lord President of the Council	Richard Crossman
Home Secretary	James Callaghan
Defence	Denis Healey
Commonwealth	George Thompson
Scotland	William Ross
Wales	George Thomas
Education and Science	Patrick Gordon Walker/Edward Short
Economic Affairs	Peter Shore
Trade	Anthony Crosland
Labour	Ray Gunter★
Housing and Local Government	Anthony Greenwood
Agriculture, Fisheries and Food	Frederick Peart/Cledwyn Hughes
Transport	Barbara Castle/Richard Marsh
Power★★	Richard Marsh/Roy Mason
Technology	Anthony Wedgwood Benn

★   To April 1968, when the new Department of Employment and Productivity was created with Barbara Castle at its head.

★★ The following year, 1969, power was subsumed as a government department within the Ministry of Technology. Technology itself disappeared in 1970 when the new Conservative Government created the Department of Trade and Industry.

Four women ministers held non-Cabinet ministerial posts: Judith Hart at Social Security; Alice Bacon, Shirley Williams and Jennie Lee at Education.

Junior ministers of the day with futures included the young David Owen and Roy Hattersley.

Also in the government at the time was John Stonehouse (1925–88). As Postmaster-General, he oversaw the introduction of second-class stamps in 1968. In 1974 he faked his own death by drowning, in Florida, apparently hoping to escape financial ruin, and start a new life in Australia. He was subsequently jailed for fraud.

Appendix 11

OLD MONEY

For those old enough to spend money in 1968, this will bring back memories; for those for whom the money of the past is another country, it will look like something out of Lewis Carroll.

In 1968 the pound sterling had 20 shillings and 240 pennies. The convention for writing pounds, shillings and pence was thus:

- £1 2s 6d = one pound, two shillings and sixpence. 'Two and six' could also be written as 2/6 and referred to as 'half a crown'.
- The penny was to be replaced in 1971 by the new decimal 'p', worth 2.4 of the old ones.
- Two halfpennies (ha'pennies) = 1 penny.
- The halfpenny was the smallest-value coin in 1968, Britain having said goodbye to the farthing (a quarter of a penny) in 1960. The ha'penny was one of the first coins withdrawn pre-decimalisation, in 1969.
- 3 pennies = threepence. Often pronounced 'threppence' or 'thruppence', and from the 1930s minted as a twelve-sided coin. This ceased to be legal tender after 1971.
- 6 pennies = sixpence, a coin often called a 'tanner'. After 1971 the sixpence was worth 2½p, but was withdrawn in 1980.

- 12 pennies = 1 shilling (a 'bob'), post-decimalisation it became 5p.
- 2 sixpences = 1 shilling; 20 shillings = £1; and 10 shillings = 'ten bob'. The 10-shilling note was withdrawn 1969–70, and the new 50p coin replaced it.
- There was also a 2-shilling coin or florin. In 1968, pre-decimalisation, the new 10p coin, of similar appearance to the florin, was introduced. The old florin finally disappeared in 1992.
- The half-crown, worth 2 shillings and sixpence (2/6), disappeared from 1969.
- In old money, values of less than £1 were usually written as shillings and pence (pennies), and in shops prices of more than a pound were often shown in the same way. Values less than a shilling would be written as pence; for example 3*d* – the *d* standing for the Latin *denarii* (coins used in Roman Britain).
- 4 shillings on a price tag was commonly written as 4/- more often than 4*s*. 4 shillings and sixpence (54 pence) would be 4/6. It was common practice in shops to mark up prices in shillings and pence, to suggest cheapness; so 19/11 (19 shillings and 11 pence) was deemed a more attractive price than £1. A guinea was 21 shillings (1 pound and 1 shilling).

Appendix 12

POLARIS

Britain's first Polaris submarine, HMS *Resolution*, was essentially a 'stretched' and modified development of the Valiant-class nuclear fleet submarines (HMS *Valiant* and HMS *Warspite*). These were the first Royal Navy submarines to have British-built reactors, Britain's first nuclear submarine, *Dreadnought*, being powered by a US reactor. *Valiant* was commissioned in 1966, *Warspite* in 1967, and they and *Resolution* served the navy into the 1990s.

Resolution as a ship's name in the navy dates back to the late seventeenth century. The nuclear submarine's most distinguished predecessor was the converted collier on which Captain James Cook made his second and third epic voyages to the Pacific (1772–79).

The Royal Navy's nuclear submarines were based at Faslane, in Scotland. Ironically it was at Faslane that the preceding HMS *Resolution*, a 1915-vintage battleship, had been broken up for scrap in 1948.

The Polaris missile which went to sea with the Royal Navy in 1968 was a two-stage, solid-fuel nuclear weapon. It had been ordered by the US Navy to replace its shipborne Regulus (an early cruise missile) and first test-fired in 1960. The Royal Navy acquired the A–3 version of Polaris, with an extended range of over 4,500km (2,800 miles) and multiple warheads. Each of its four submarines carried sixteen Polaris missiles.

The US Navy went on to deploy the more powerful Poseidon, but Britain stayed with Polaris, updating the missile in the 1980s with the Chevaline system. This had two warheads plus decoys, and was designed to increase the missile's ability to penetrate improving anti-missile defences. Polaris continued in service until the 1990s.

HMS *Resolution* was decommissioned in 1994, with the advent of four new Vanguard-class submarines armed with US Trident missiles.

Appendix 13

DEATHS IN 1968

A personal selection from the obituary columns

W.E. Johns (b. 1893)	author, creator of Biggles
R.J. Yeatman (b. 1897)	humorous writer (*1066 and All That*)
Princess Marina (b. 1906)	Duchess of Kent
Mervyn Peake (b. 1911)	novelist
Tony Hancock (b. 1934)	comedian
Upton Sinclair (b. 1878)	novelist
Basil Sydney (b. 1894)	actor
Enid Blyton (b. 1897)	author
Bud Flanagan (b. 1896)	comedian
Jess Willard (b. 1881)	US boxer
Randolph Churchill (b. 1911)	journalist, MP, son of Sir Winston
Jim Clark (b. 1936)	racing driver
Finlay Currie (b. 1878)	actor
Dan Duryea (b. 1907)	actor
Tallulah Bankhead (b. 1903)	actress
Anthony Asquith (b. 1902)	film-maker
John Steinbeck (b. 1902)	novelist
Sir Donald Wolfit (b. 1902)	actor

Martin Luther King Jr (b. 1929)	civil rights leader
Robert F. Kennedy (b. 1925)	politician
Helen Keller (b. 1880)	disability pioneer
Dorothy Gish (b. 1898)	actress
Frankie Lymon (b. 1942)	pop singer
Yuri Gagarin (b. 1934)	cosmonaut
Ramon Navarro (b. 1899)	actor
Trygve Lie (b. 1896)	UN Secretary General
Lise Meitner (b. 1878)	physicist
Otto Hahn (b. 1879)	physicist

Further Reading

Ali, Tariq, *Street-Fighting Years: An Autobiography of the Sixties*, London: Verso, 2005.

Birmingham, Stephen, *Jacqueline Bouvier Kennedy Onassis*, London: Fontana, 1979.

Broackes, Victoria and Marsh, Geoffrey (eds), *You Say You Want a Revolution? Records and Rebels, 1966–1970*, London: V&A Publishing, 2016.

Busch, Peter, *All the way with JFK? Britain, the US, and the Vietnam War*, Oxford: Oxford University Press, 2003.

Clarke, Arthur C., *2001: A Space Odyssey*, London: Hutchinson, 1968.

Davies, Hunter, *The Beatles*, London: Heinemann, 1968, second revised edition, London: McGraw-Hill, 1986.

Faith, Nicholas, *A Very Different Country*, London: Sinclair-Stevenson, 2002.

Fisher, John, *Tony Hancock*, London: HarperCollins, 2008.

Fowler, David, *Youth Culture in Britain c. 1920–c. 1970*, London: Palgrave Macmillan, 2008.

Friedan, Betty, *The Feminine Mystique*, New York: W. W. Norton, 1963.

Green, Felicity with Stemp, Sinty, *Sex, Sense and Nonsense: Felicity Green on the 60s Fashion Scene*, Woodbridge: ACC Editions, 2014.

Green, Jonathon, *All Dressed Up: The Sixties and the Counter-Culture*, London: Jonathan Cape, 1998.

Kinealy, Christine, *War and Peace: Ireland since the 1960s*, London: Reaktion Books, 2010.

Kray, Ronnie, *My Story*, London: Sidgwick & Jackson, 1993.

Lennon, Cynthia, *John*, London: Hodder & Stoughton, 2005.

Ling, Peter J., *Martin Luther King, Jr*, Abingdon: Routledge, 2002.

Lovejoy, Joe, *Bestie: A Portrait of a Legend*, London: Pan Macmillan, 2013

Marr, Andrew, *The History of Modern Britain*, London: Macmillan, 2007.

Marwick, Arthur, *The Sixties: Cultural Revolution in Britain, France, Italy and the United States c. 1958–1974*, Oxford: Oxford University Press, 1998.

Opie, Robert, *The 1960s Scrapbook*, London: New Cavendish Books, 2000.

Paterson, Peter, *Tired and Emotional: The Life of Lord George-Brown*, London: Chatto & Windus, 1993.

Pimlott, Ben, *Harold Wilson*, London: HarperCollins, 1992, revised edition 2016.

Rayner, Geoffrey, Chamberlain, Richard & Stapleton, Annamarie, *Pop! Design, Culture, Fashion 1956–1976*, Woodbridge: ACC Editions, 2012.

Reynolds, Bruce, *Crossing the Line: The Autobiography of a Thief*, London: Virgin, 2003.

Ross, Kristin, *May 1968 and its Afterlives*, Chicago: University of Chicago Press, 2002.

Rowbotham, Sheila, *The Past is Before Us: Feminism in Action Since the 1960s*, London: Pandora Press, 1989.

Sampson, Anthony, *The Essential Anatomy of Britain*, London: Hodder & Stoughton 1992, and others in the author's *Anatomy of Britain* series.

Sandbrook, Dominic, *White Heat: A History of Britain in the Swinging Sixties*, London: Little, Brown, 2006.

Seton-Watson, Hugh, *The Imperialist Revolutionaries: World Communism in the 1960s and 1970s*, London: Hutchinson, 1980.

Turnock, Robert, *Television and Consumer Culture: Britain and the Transformation of Modernity*, London: I.B. Tauris, 2007.

Updike, John, *Couples*, London: André Deutsch, 1968.

Walford, Jonathan, *Sixties Fashion: From Less is More to Youthquake*, London: Thames & Hudson, 2013.

Wilson, Harold, *The Labour Government, 1964–1970: A Personal Record*, London: Weidenfeld & Nicolson and Michael Joseph, 1971.

Wolin, Richard, *The Wind from the East: French Intellectuals, the Cultural Revolution, and the Legacy of the 1960s*, Princeton: Princeton University Press, 2012.

Ziegler, Philip, *Wilson: The Authorised Life*, London: Weidenfeld & Nicholson, 1993.

Index